MAGIKA

THE ART OF MÉLANIE DELON

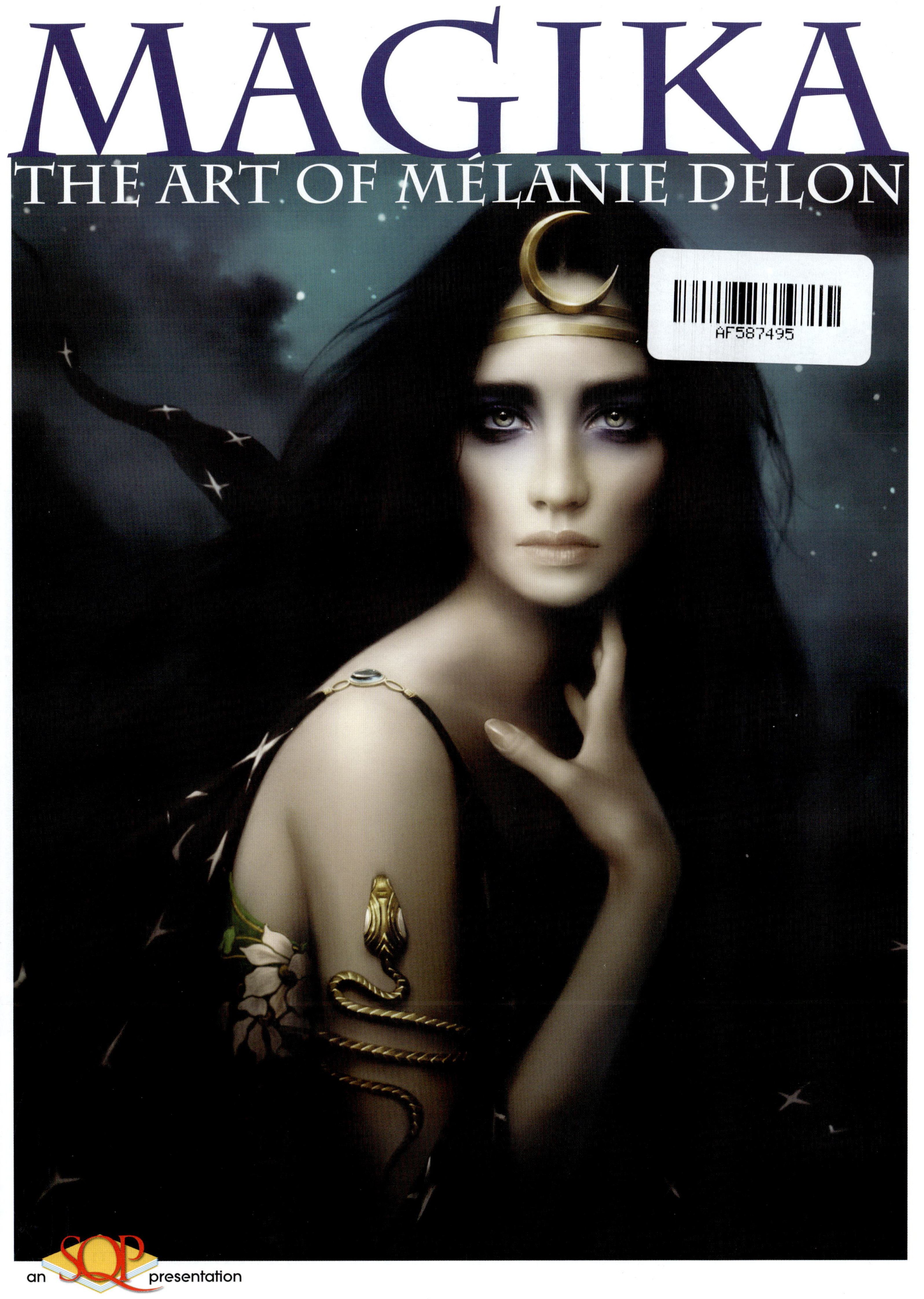

an SQP presentation

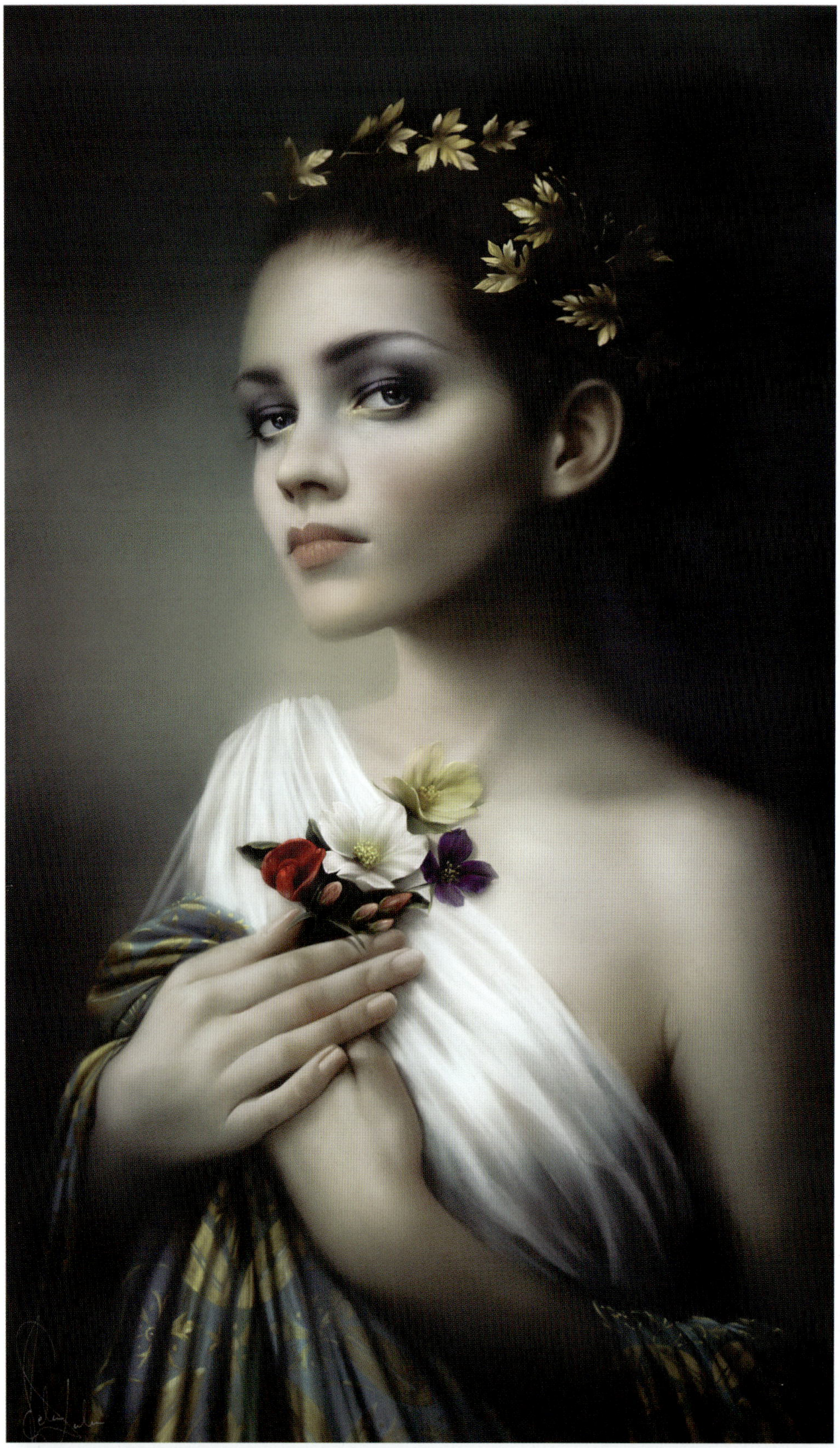

Born in Paris, France in 1980, Mélanie studied archaeology, history of art, and game design before discovering digital painting in 2005, she has been enthralled by it ever since. Using primarily Photoshop and Painter, along with a drawing tablet, she creates stunningly, realistic digital portraits which are both mysterious and emotive.

Her fantasy paintings have featured in many publications worldwide and won her a variety of awards. Mélanie is an avid Science Fiction and Fantasy reader, her favourite authors include; Philip K. Dick, J.R.R. Tolkien and Terry Pratchett.

Some of her drawings are inspired by music, others by movies and everyday situations. All of her characters have their own stories – it helps her to give them life.

Mélanie's work has been selected for Spectrum and she is a regular contributor to Imagine FX magazine. She has several art books of her beautiful work published.

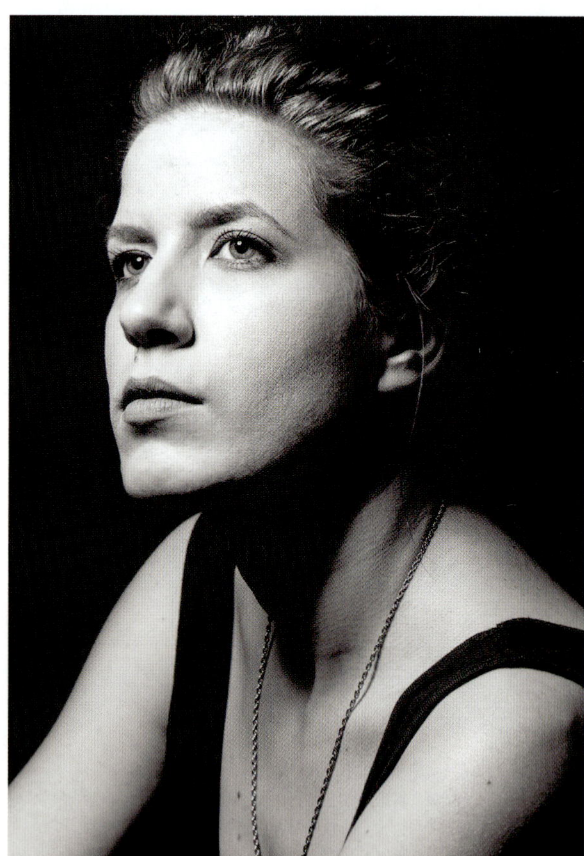

For the very latest works by Mélanie, go to www.melaniedelon.com

Magika - The Art of Mélanie Delon

Book design by Grassy Knoll Studios.

Published by SQP Inc. - PO Box 248 - Columbus NJ 08022

Sal Quartuccio & Bob Keenan - Publishers

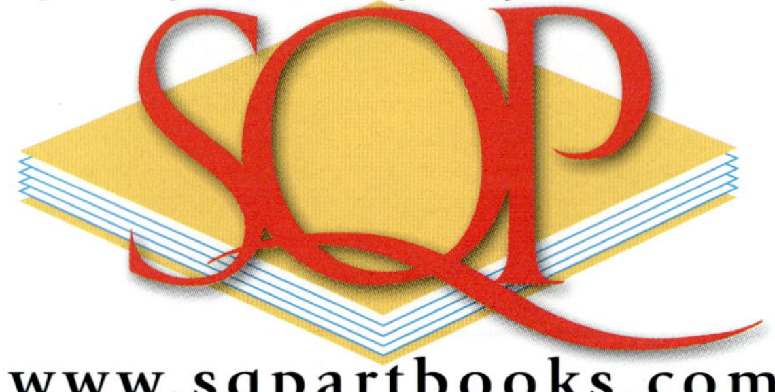

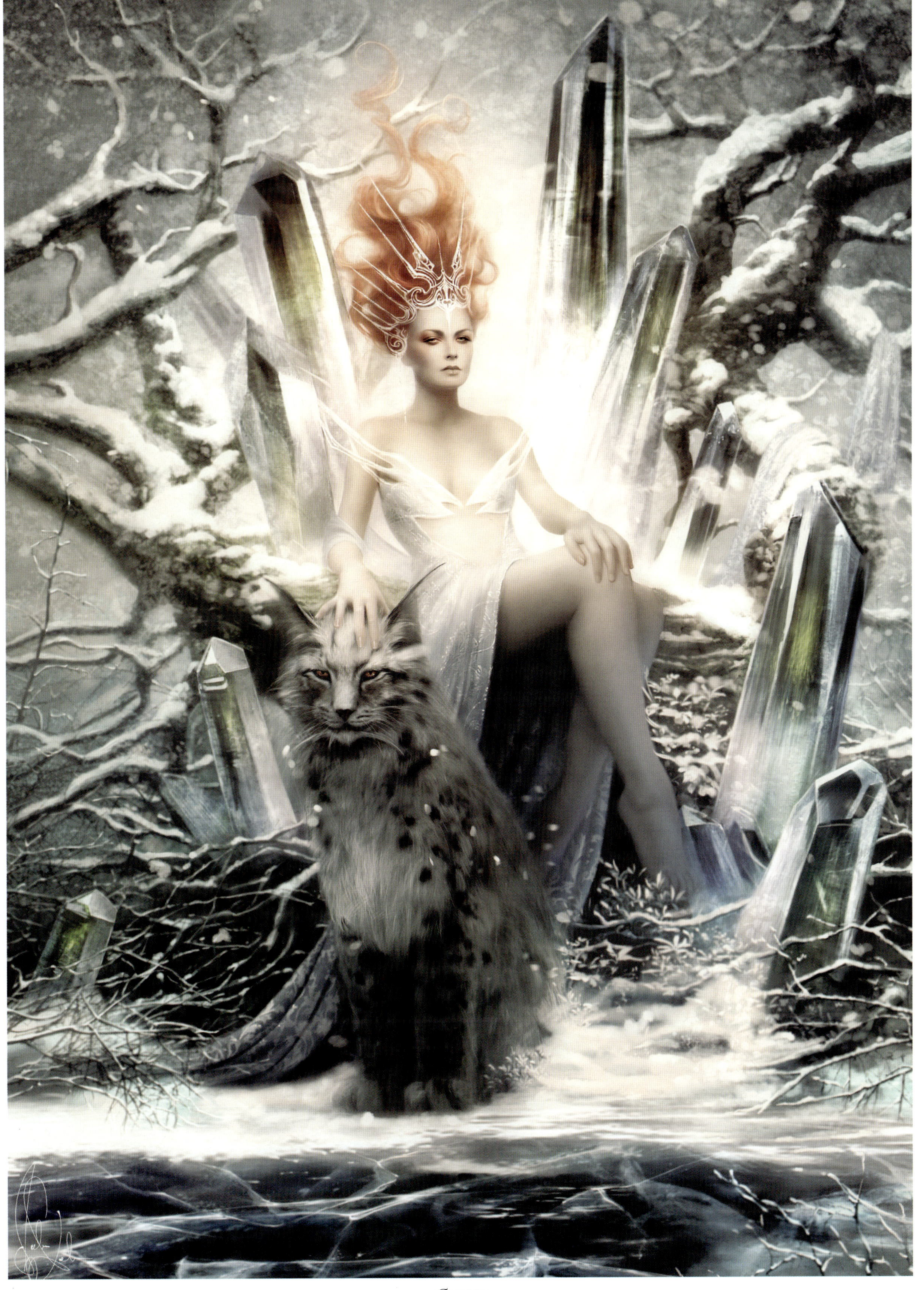

Crystal

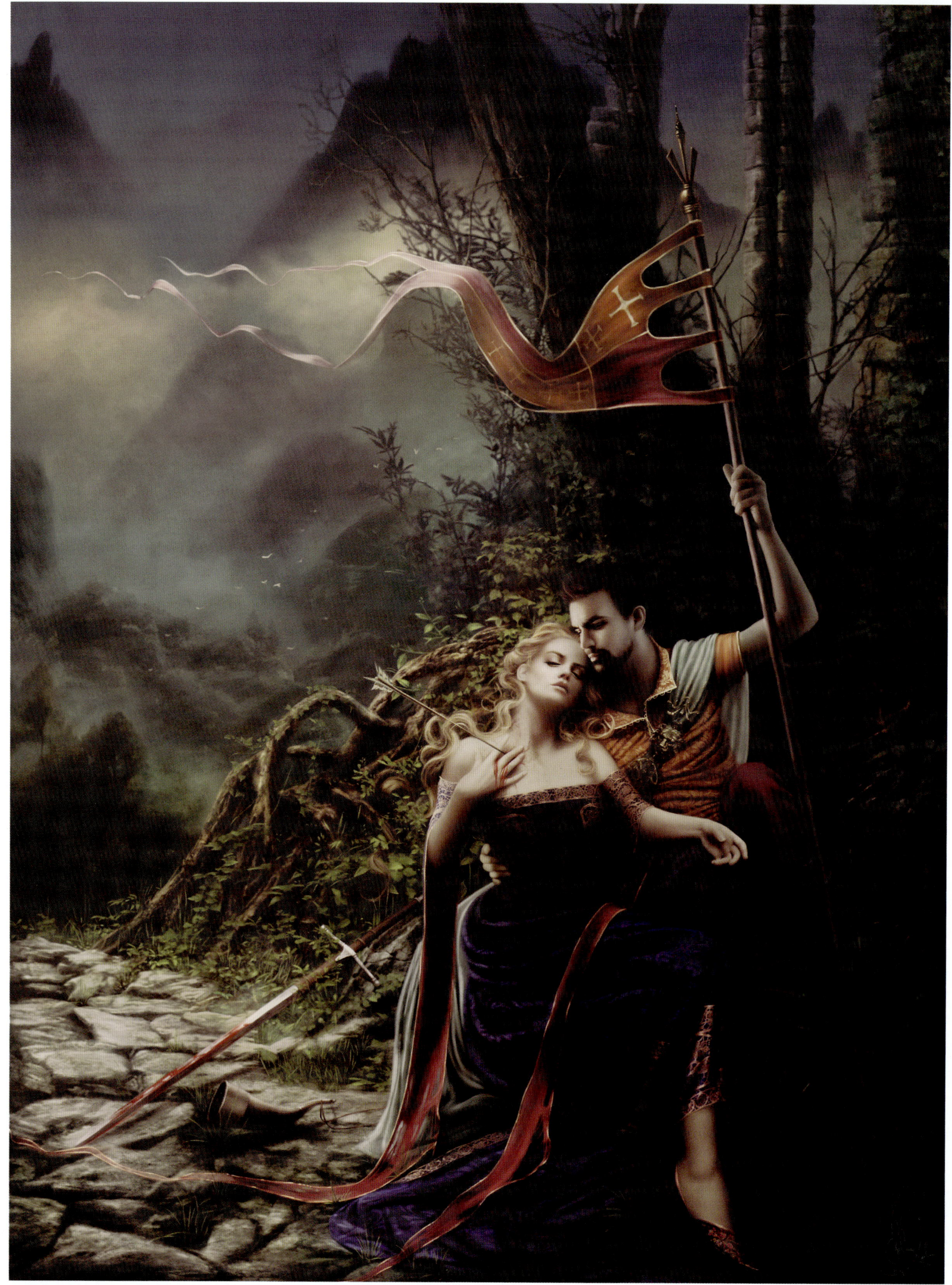

Rescue me

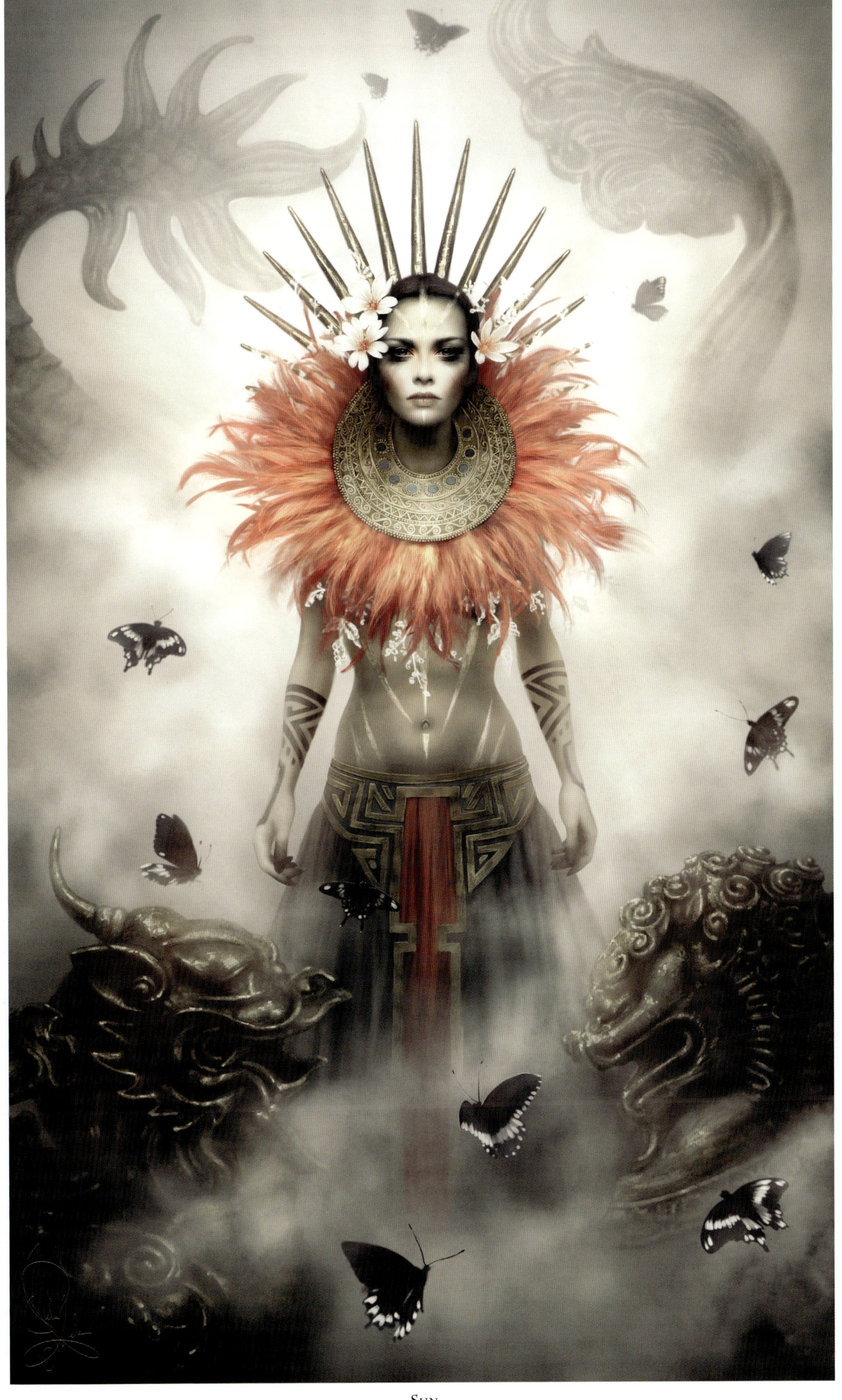

Sun

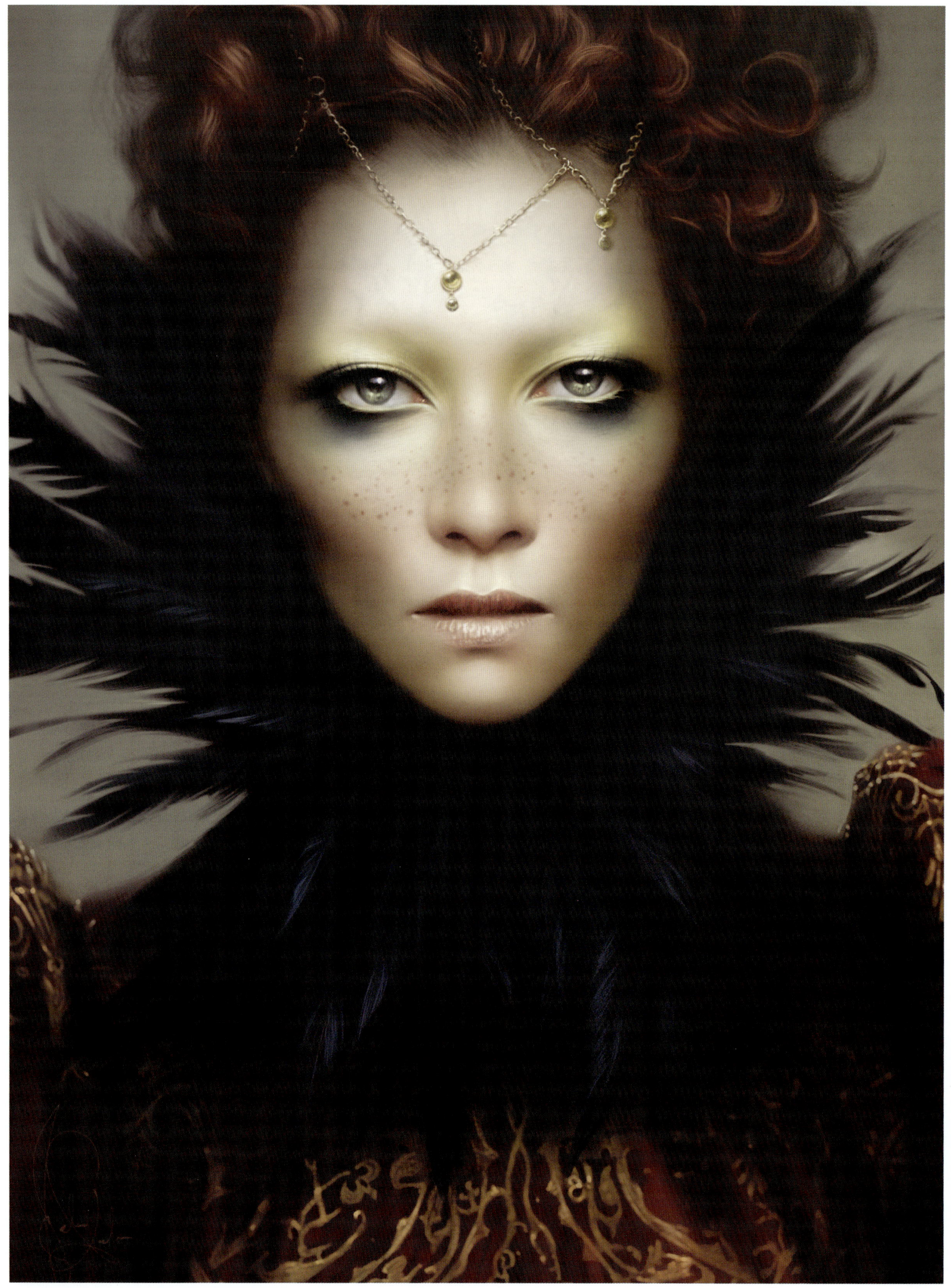

Jane

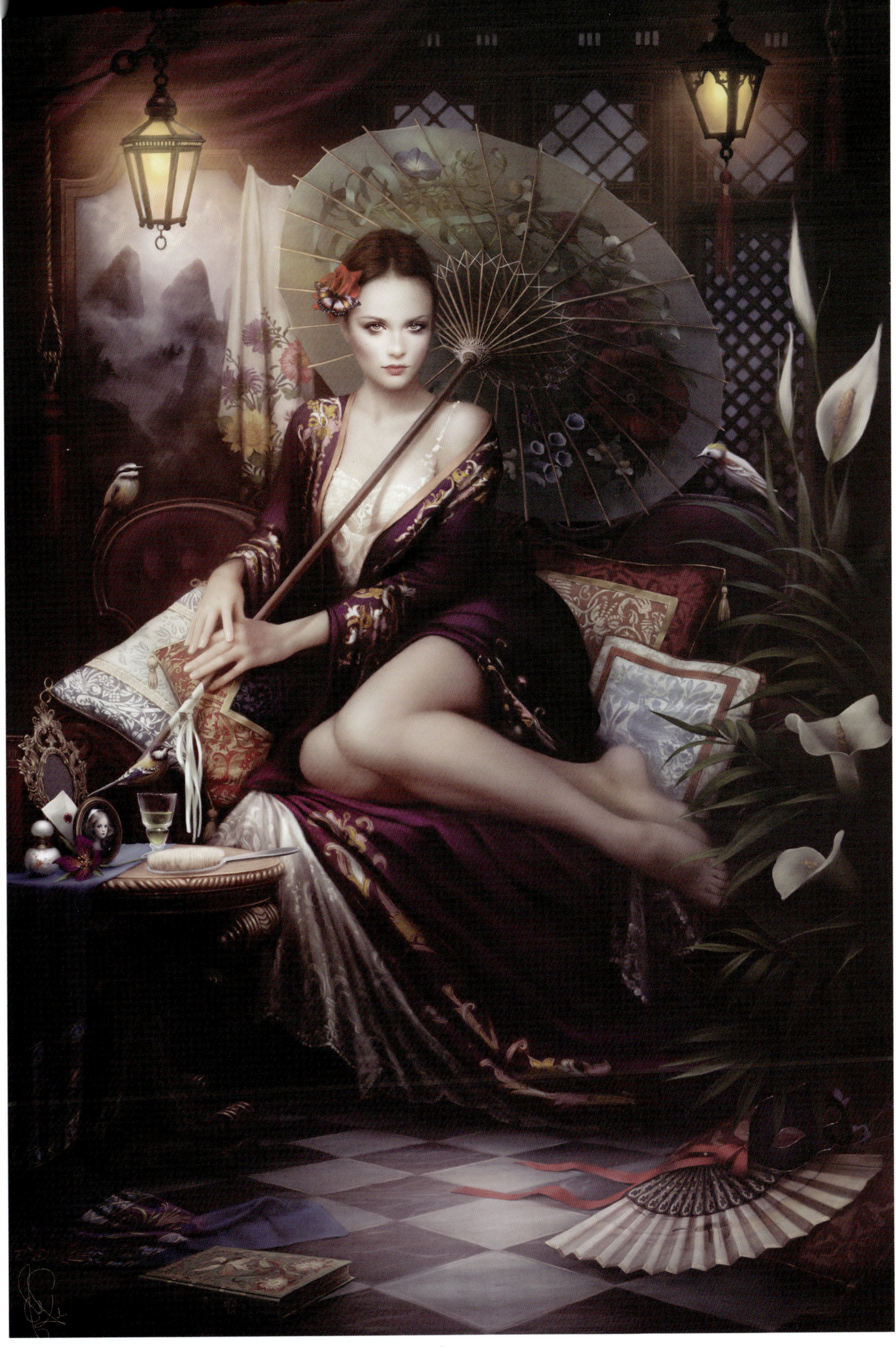

Anis

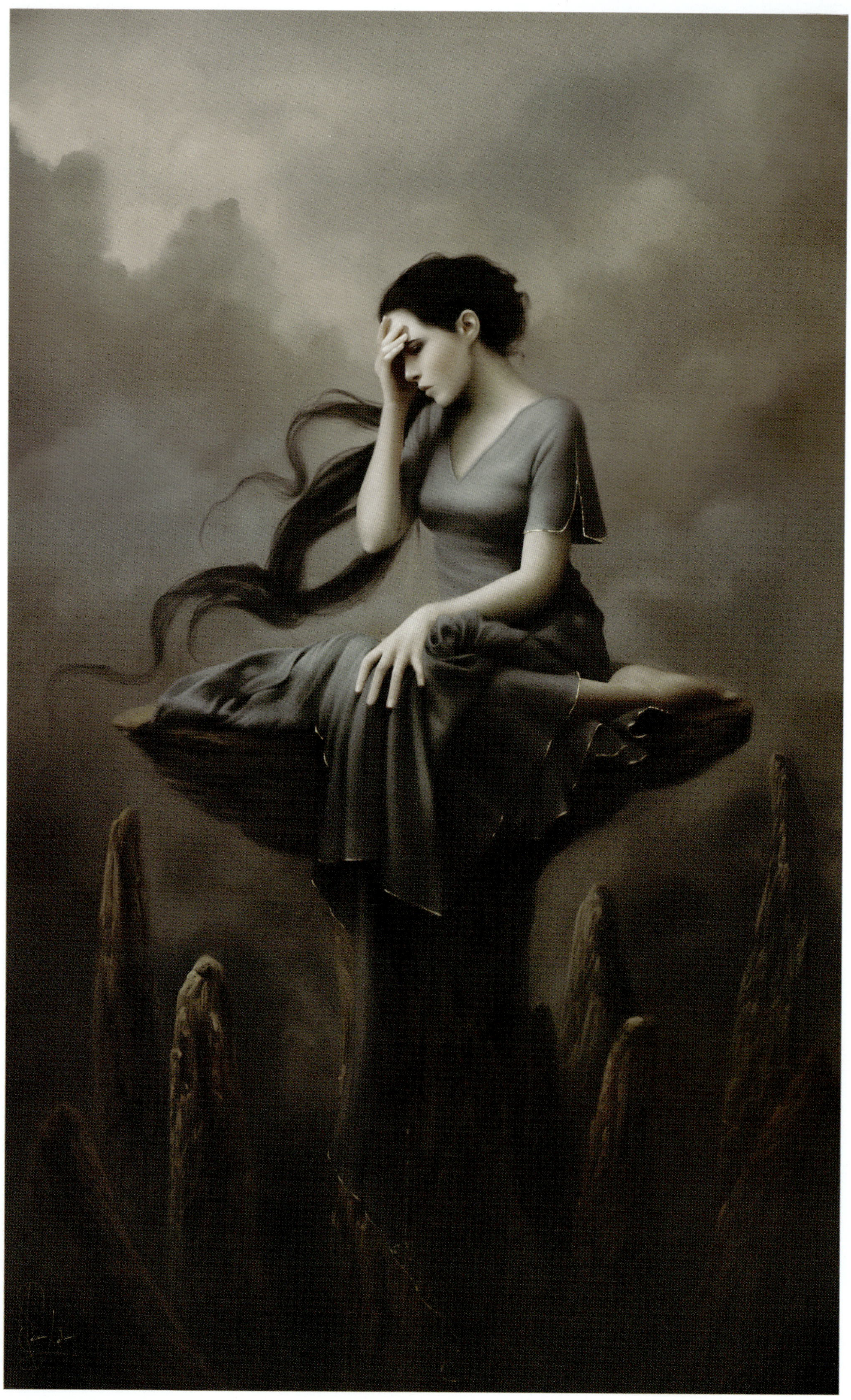

The End of Days

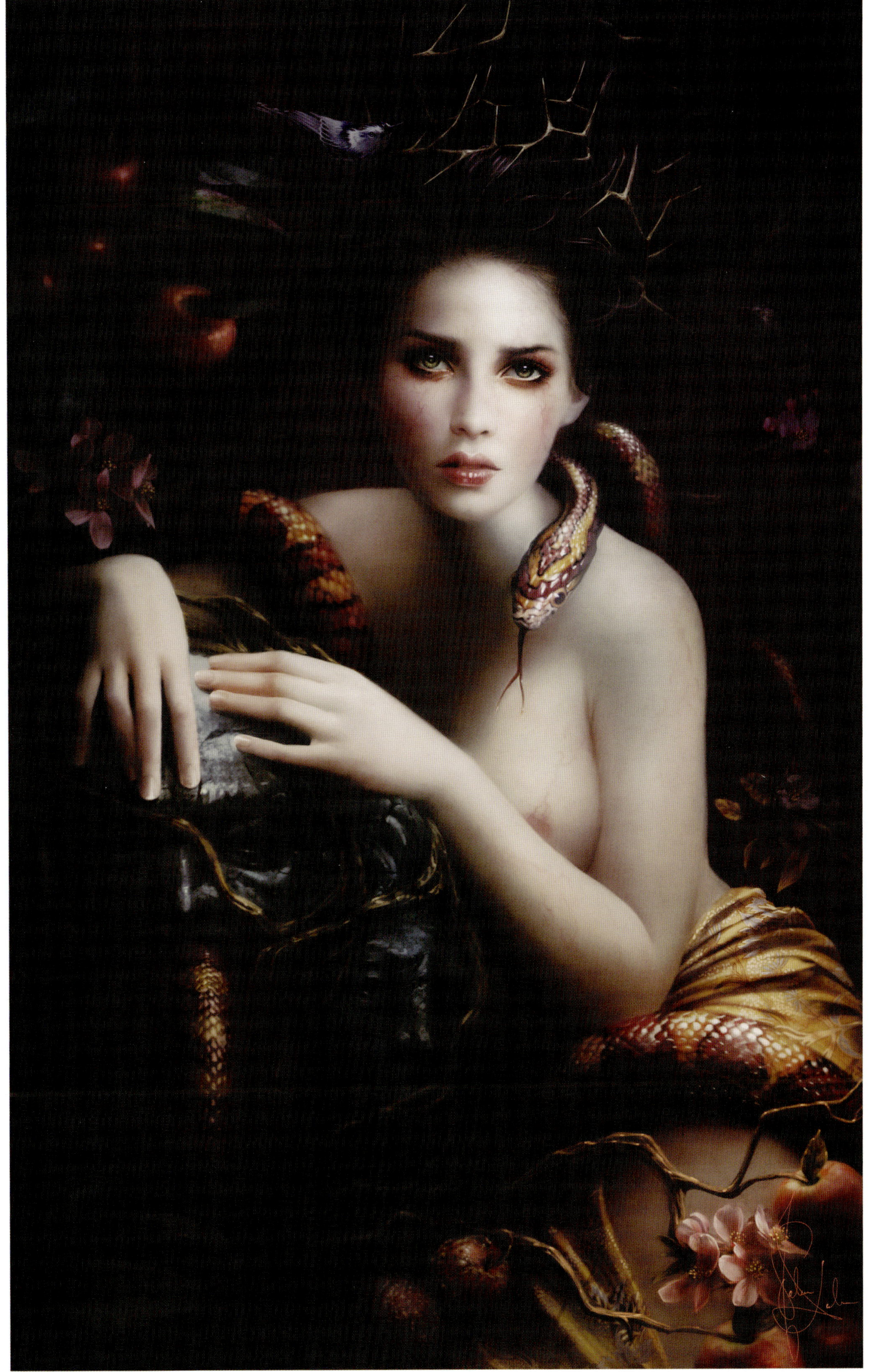

Eva

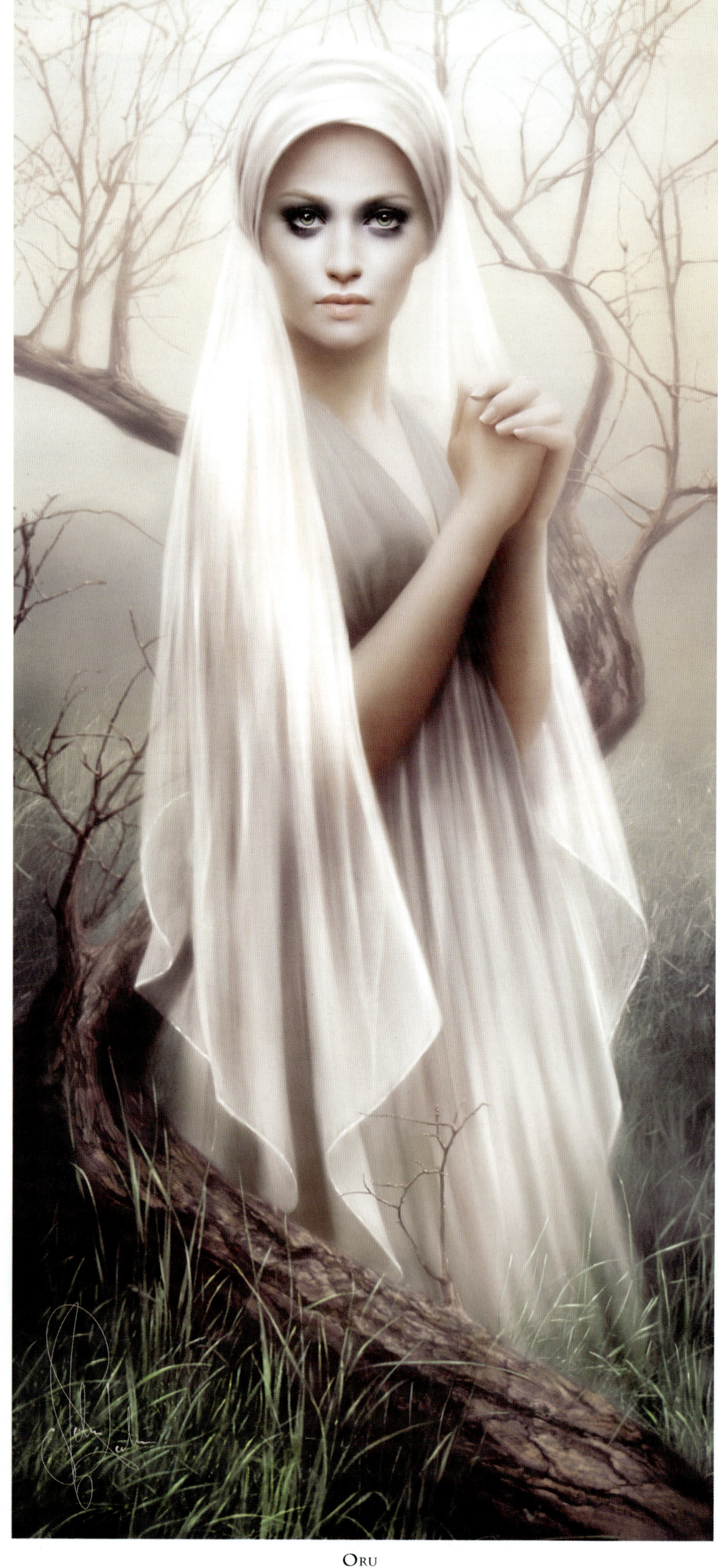

Oru

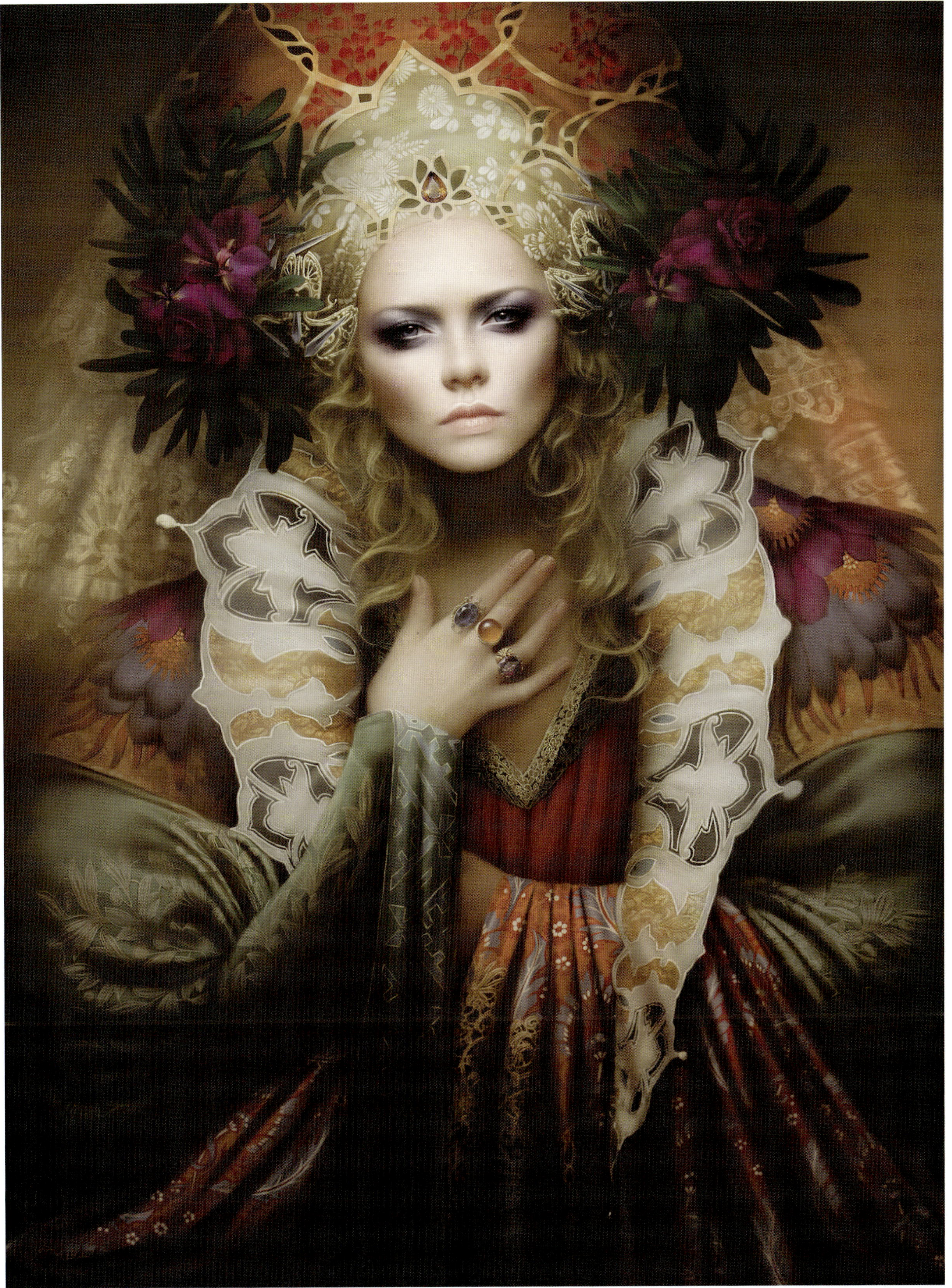

Witness

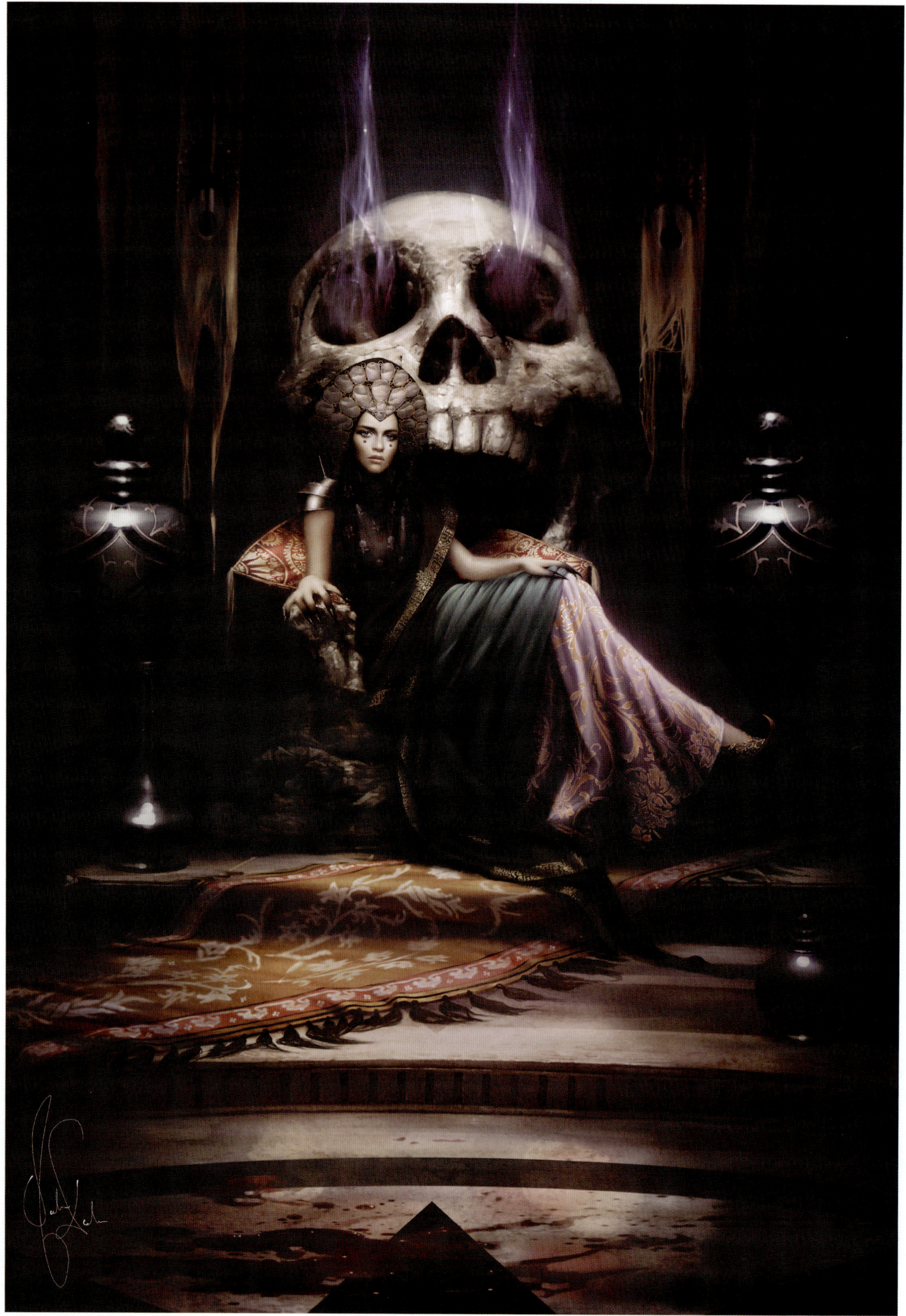

Throne

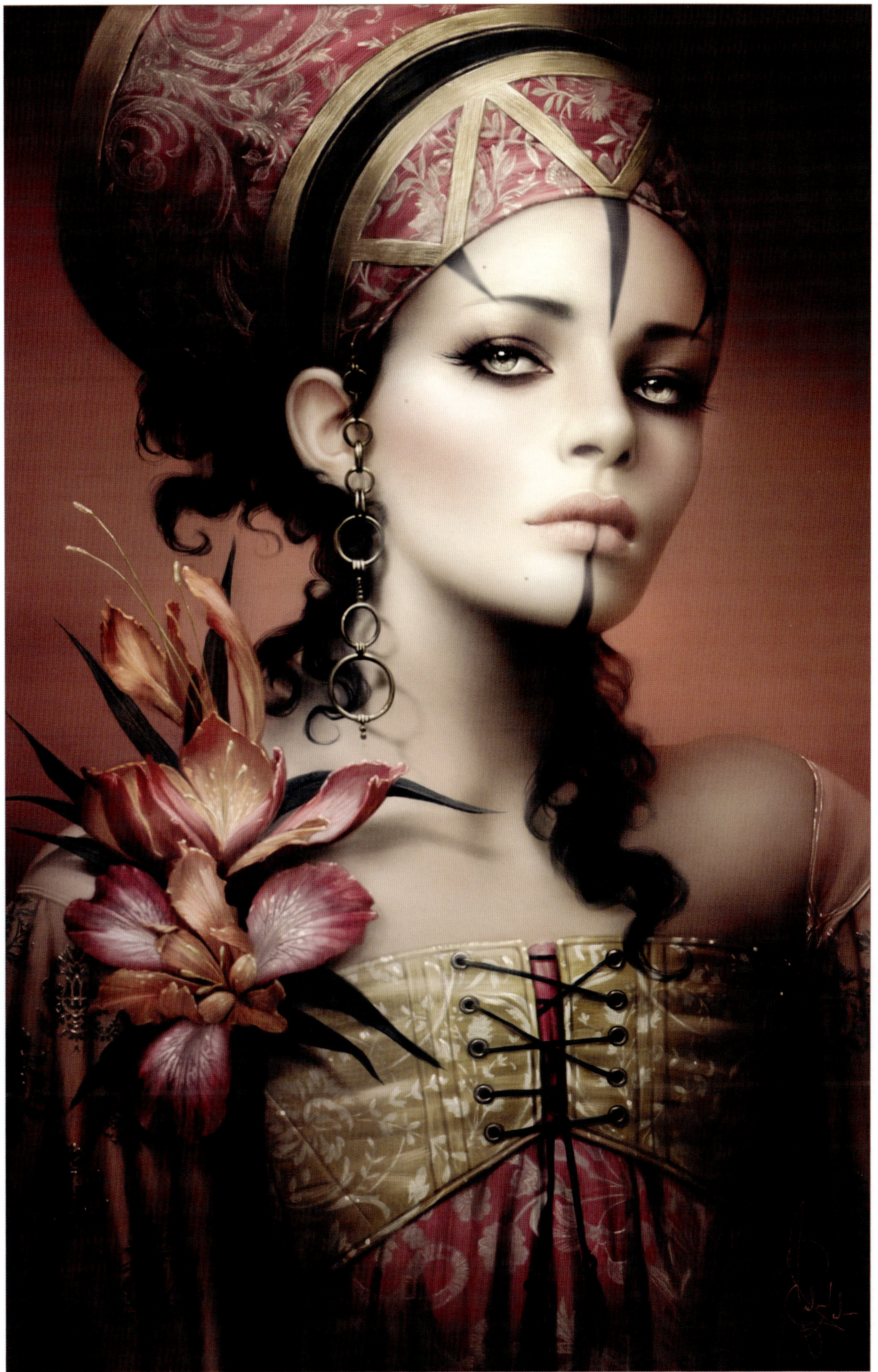

Glow

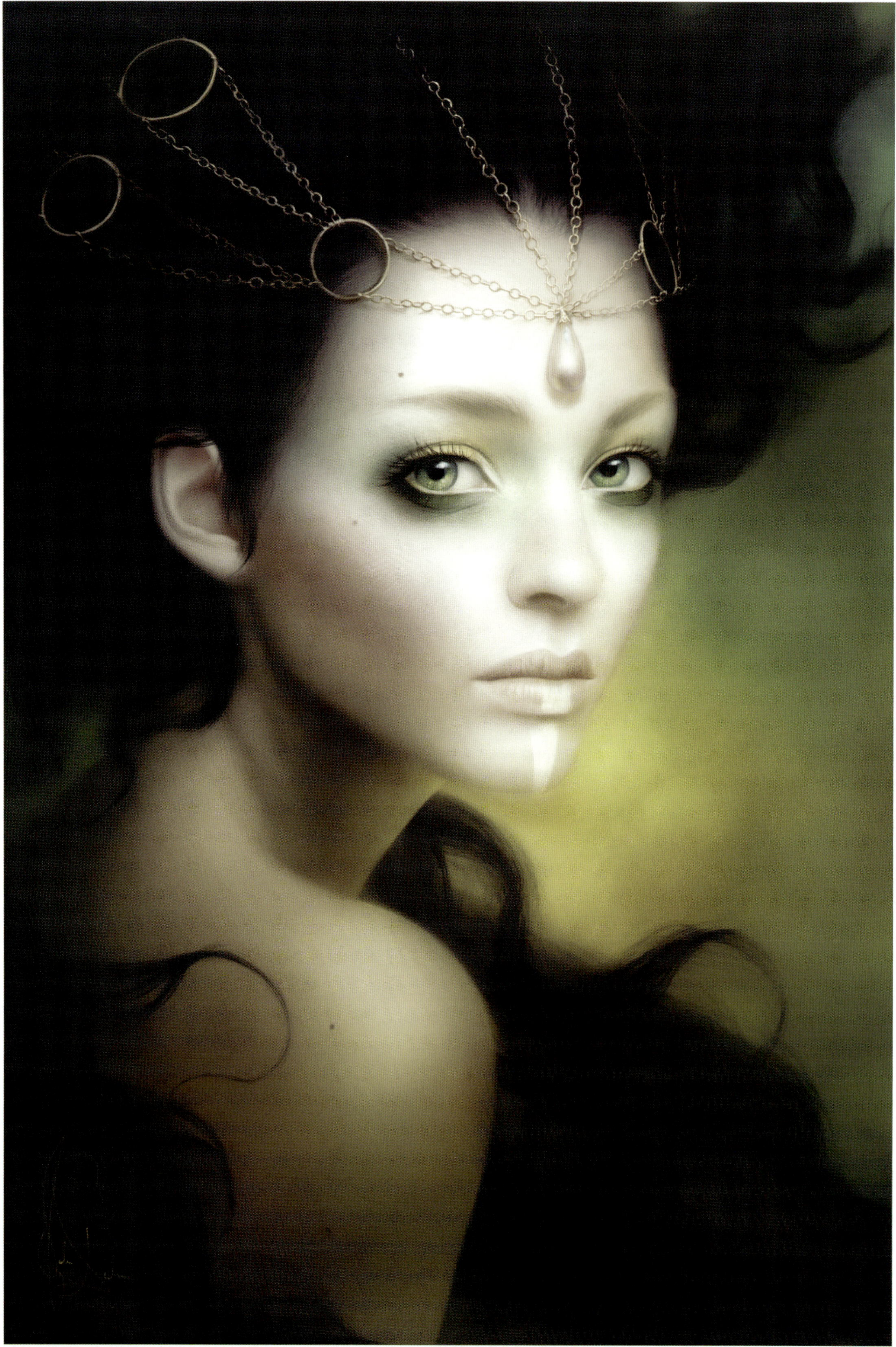

June

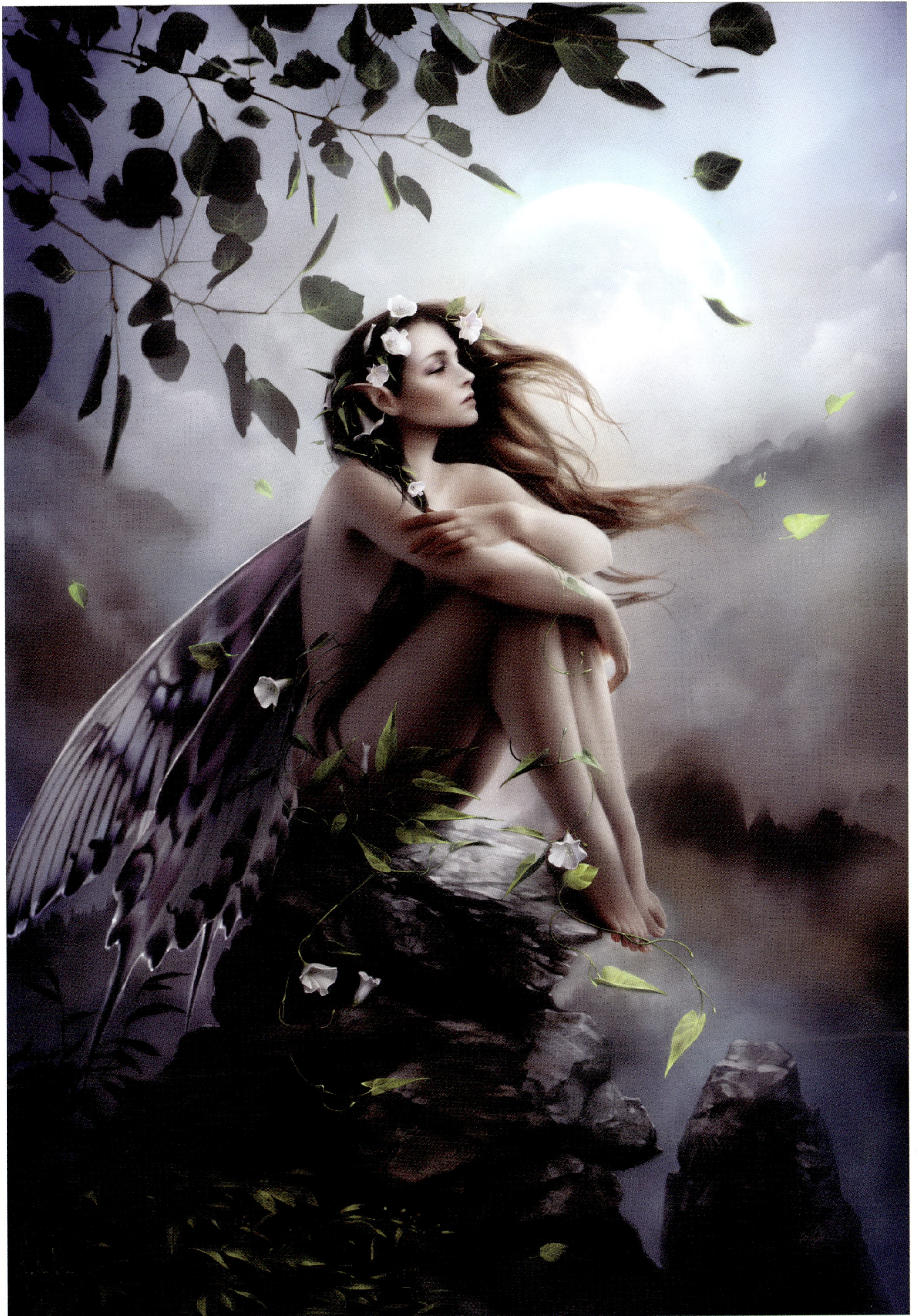

Isra

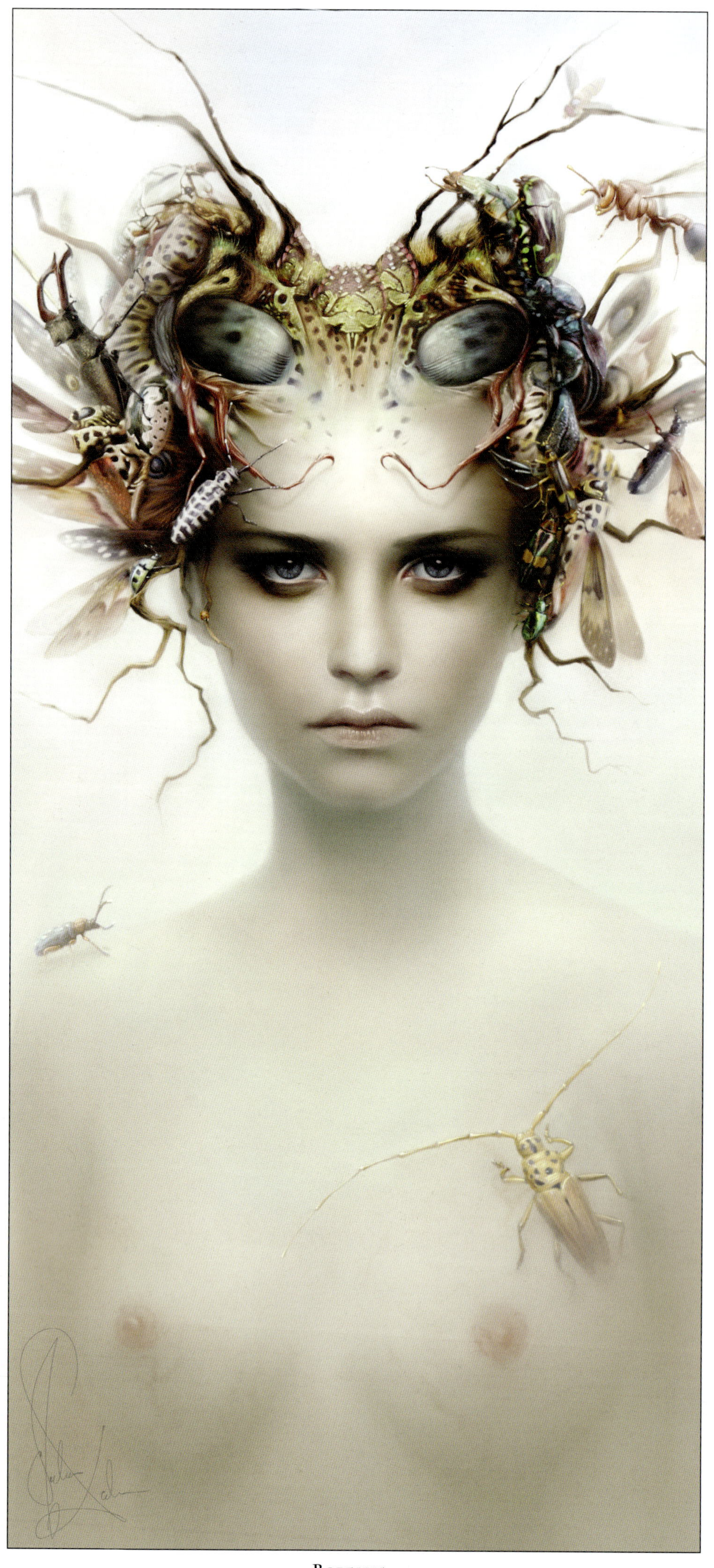

Borealis

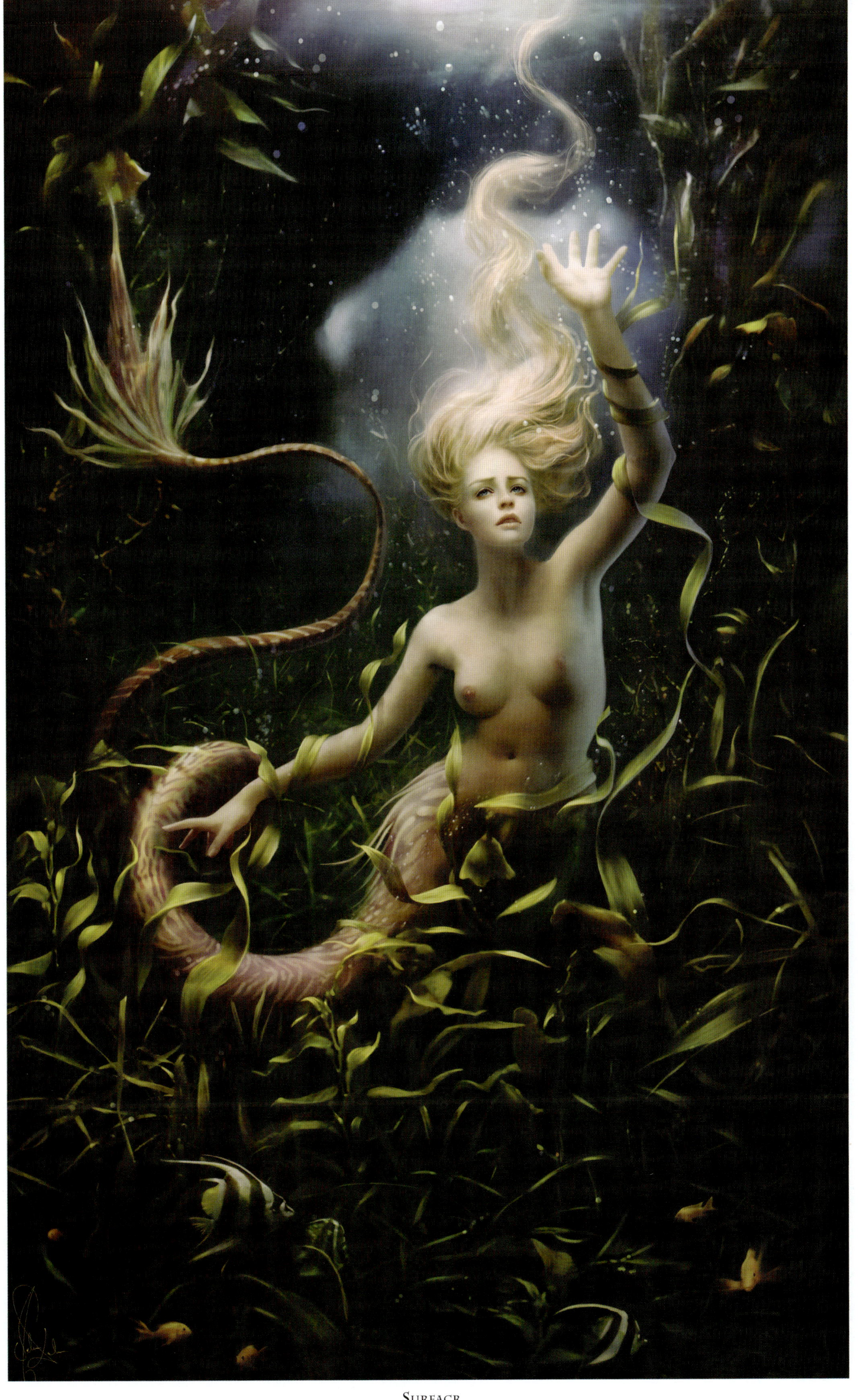

Surfacr

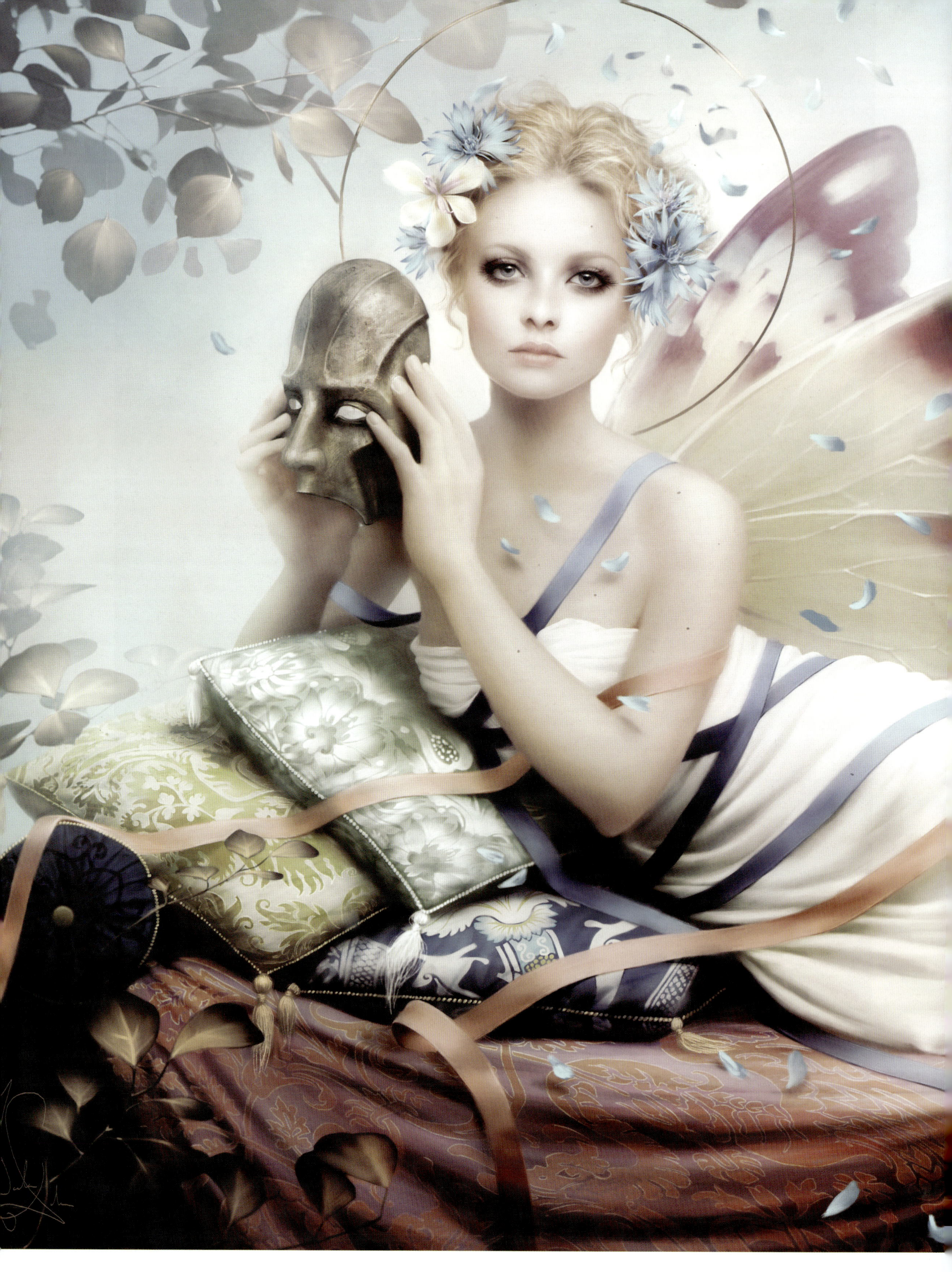

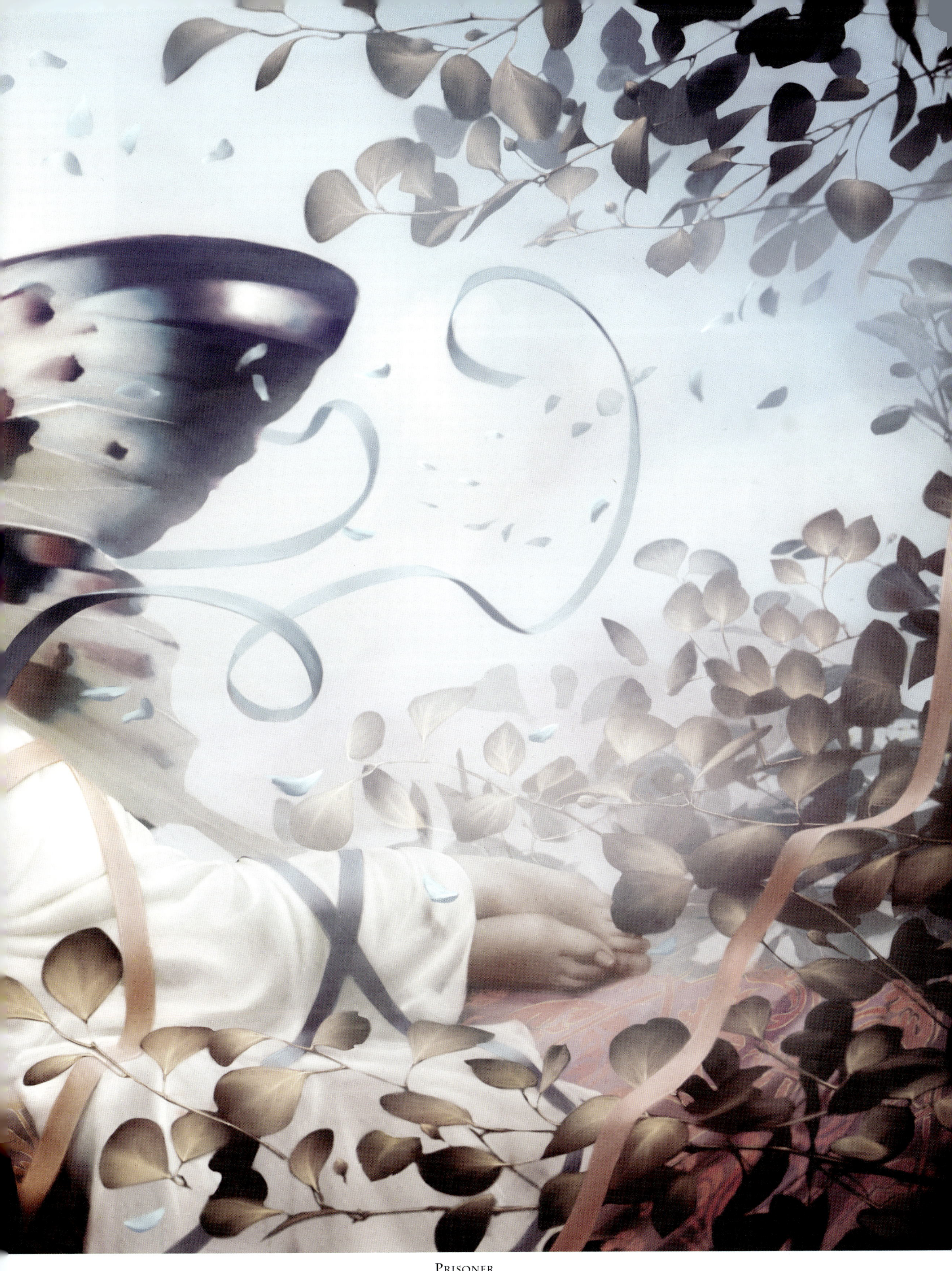

Prisoner

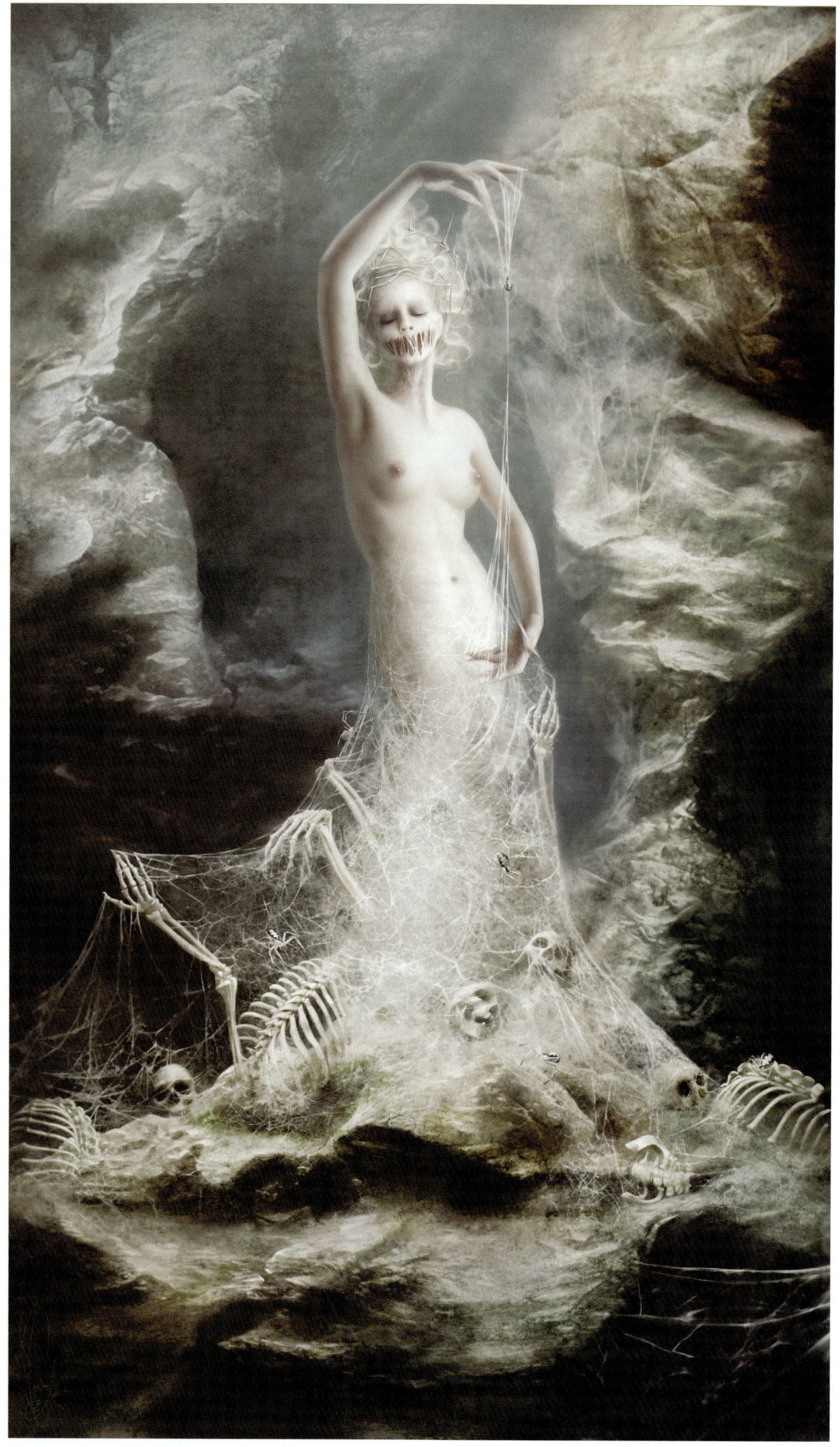

Toile

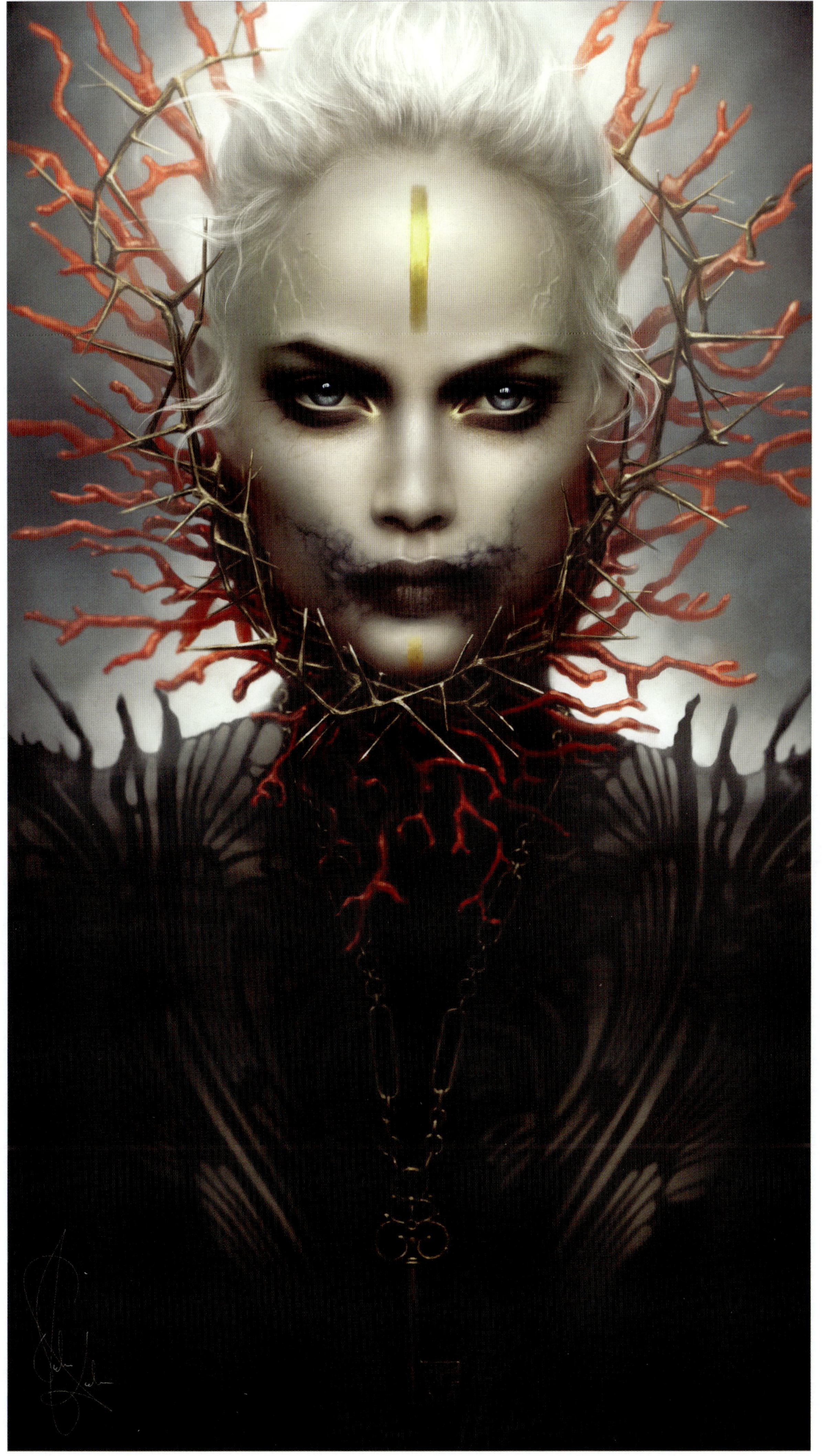

My Eyes

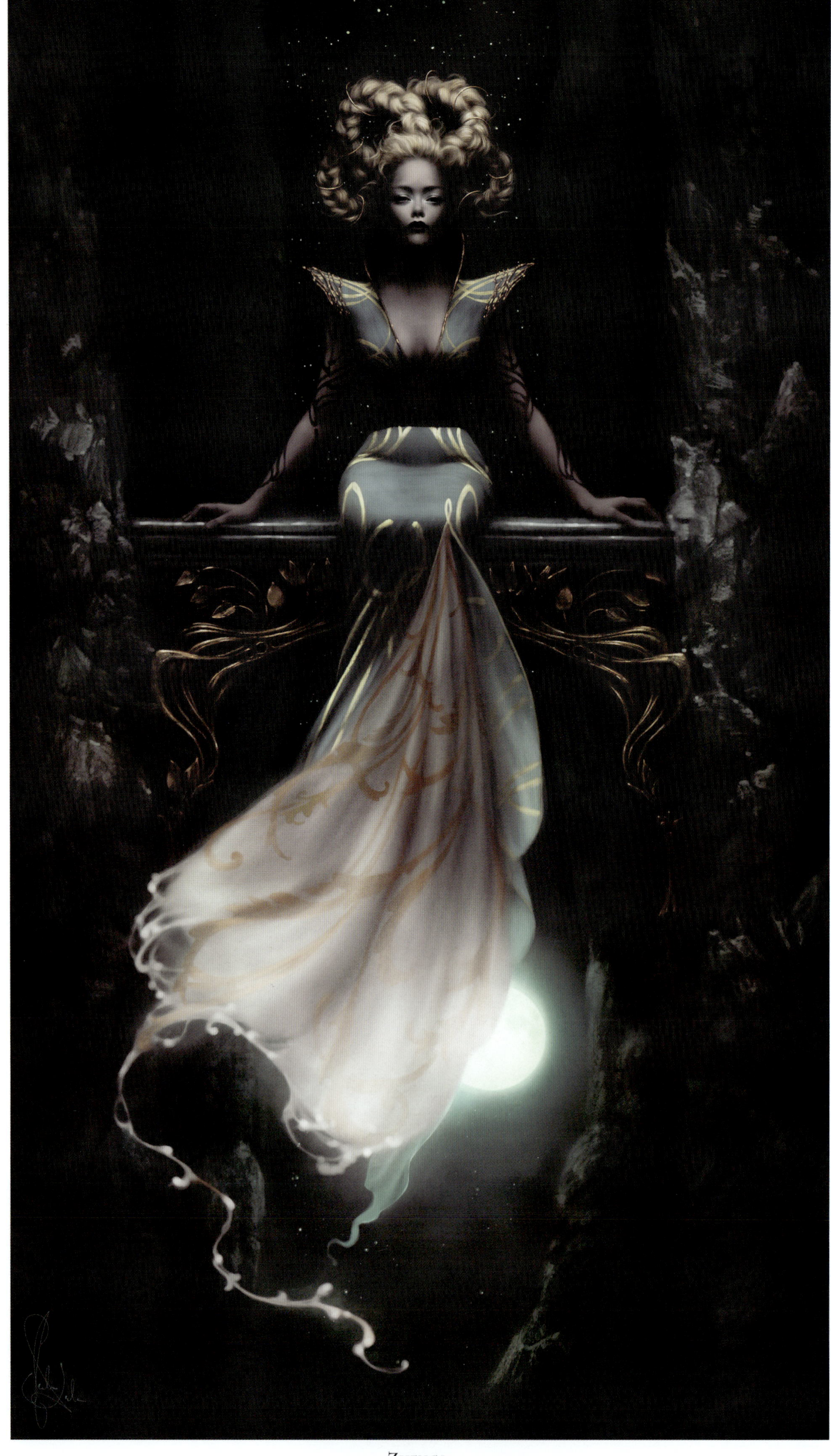

Zhenga

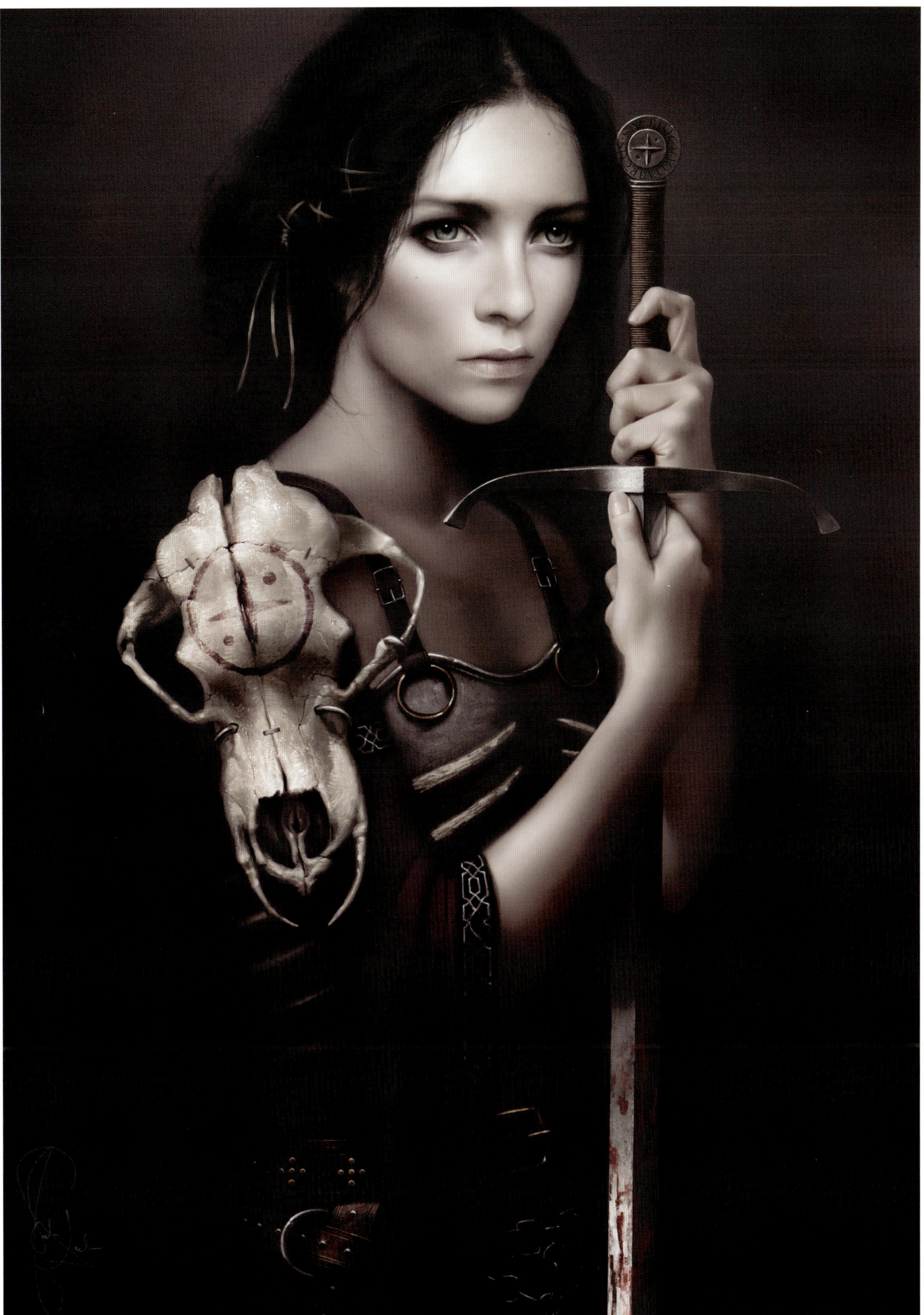

Sacrifice

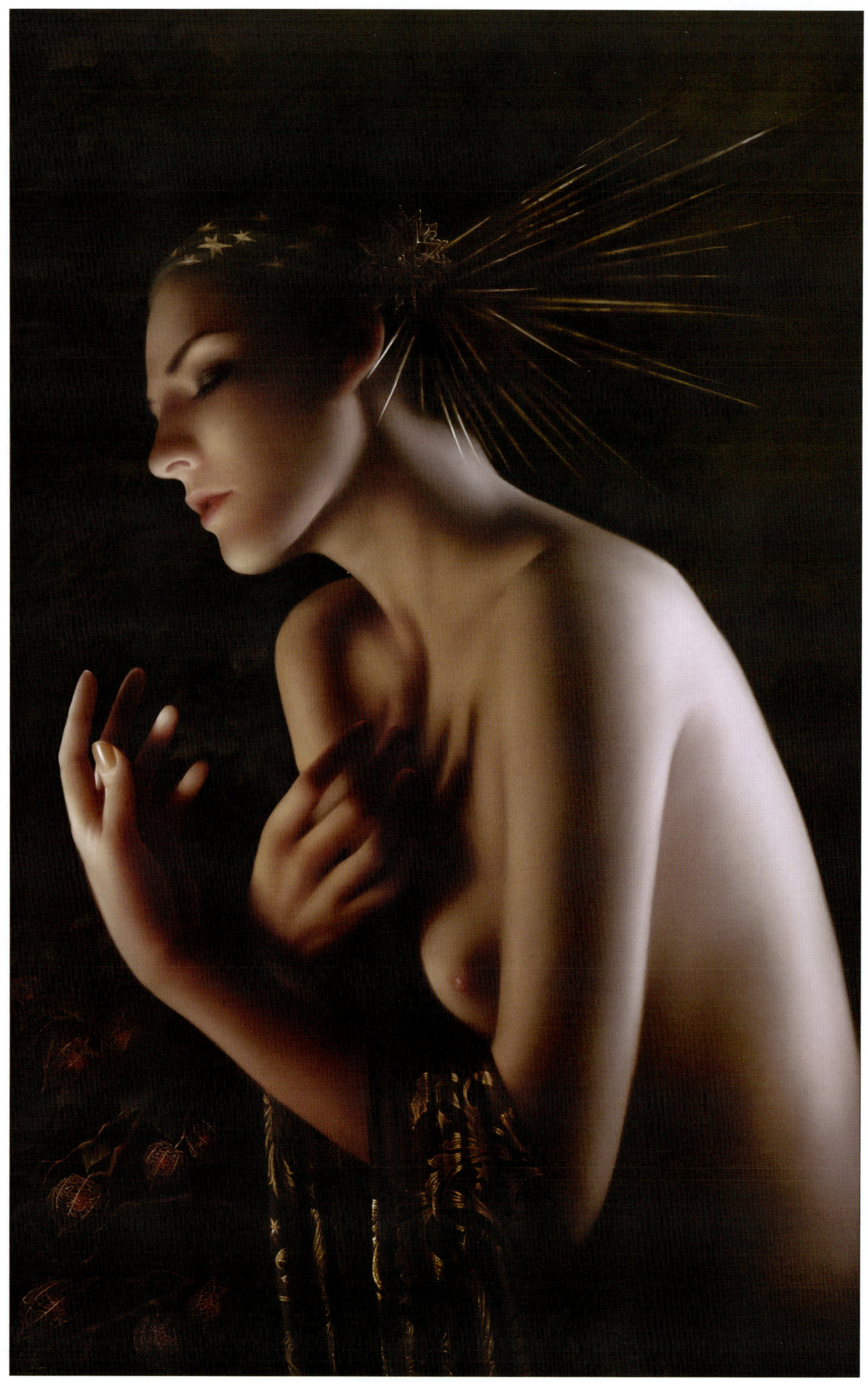

The Seer

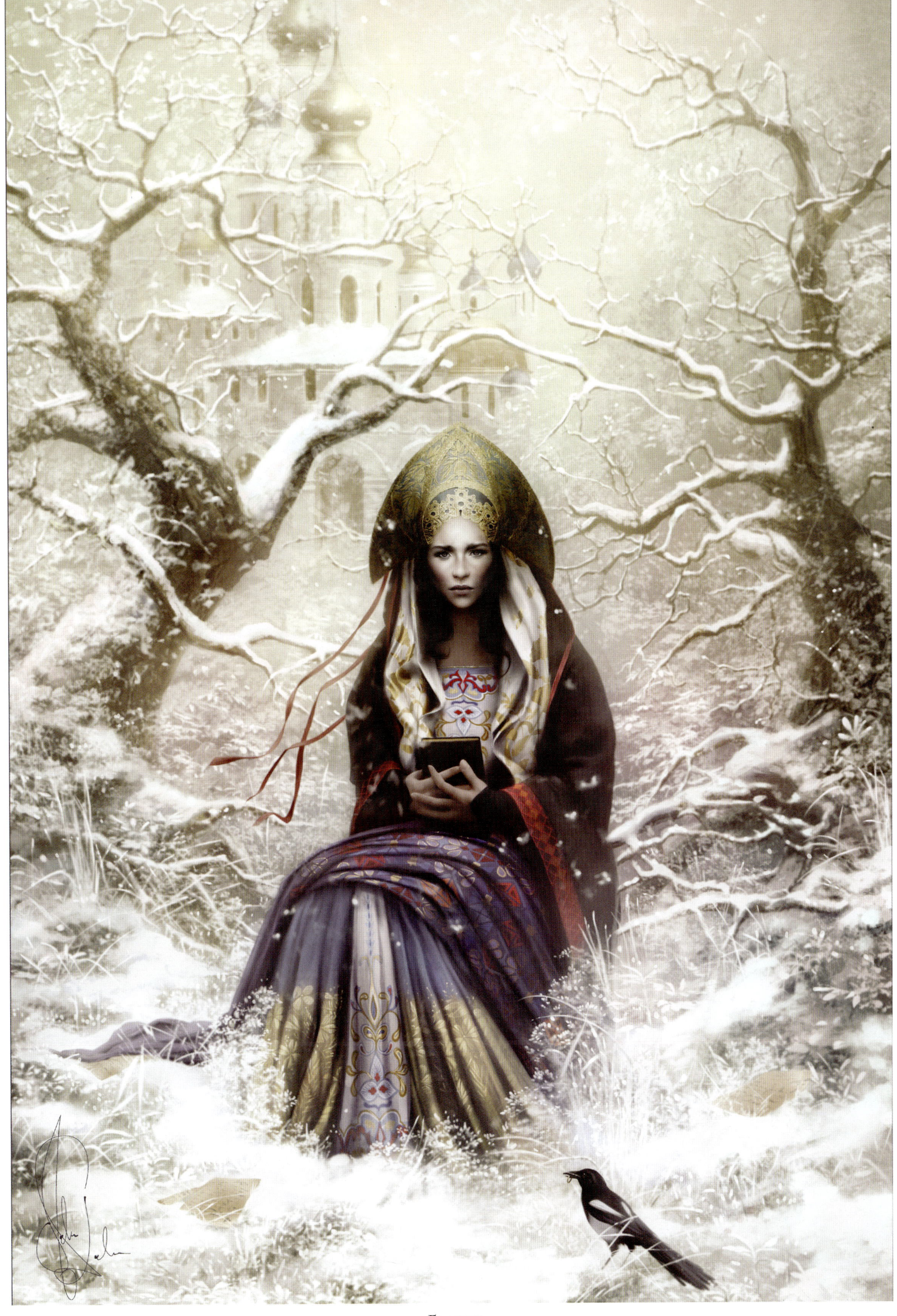

Forever

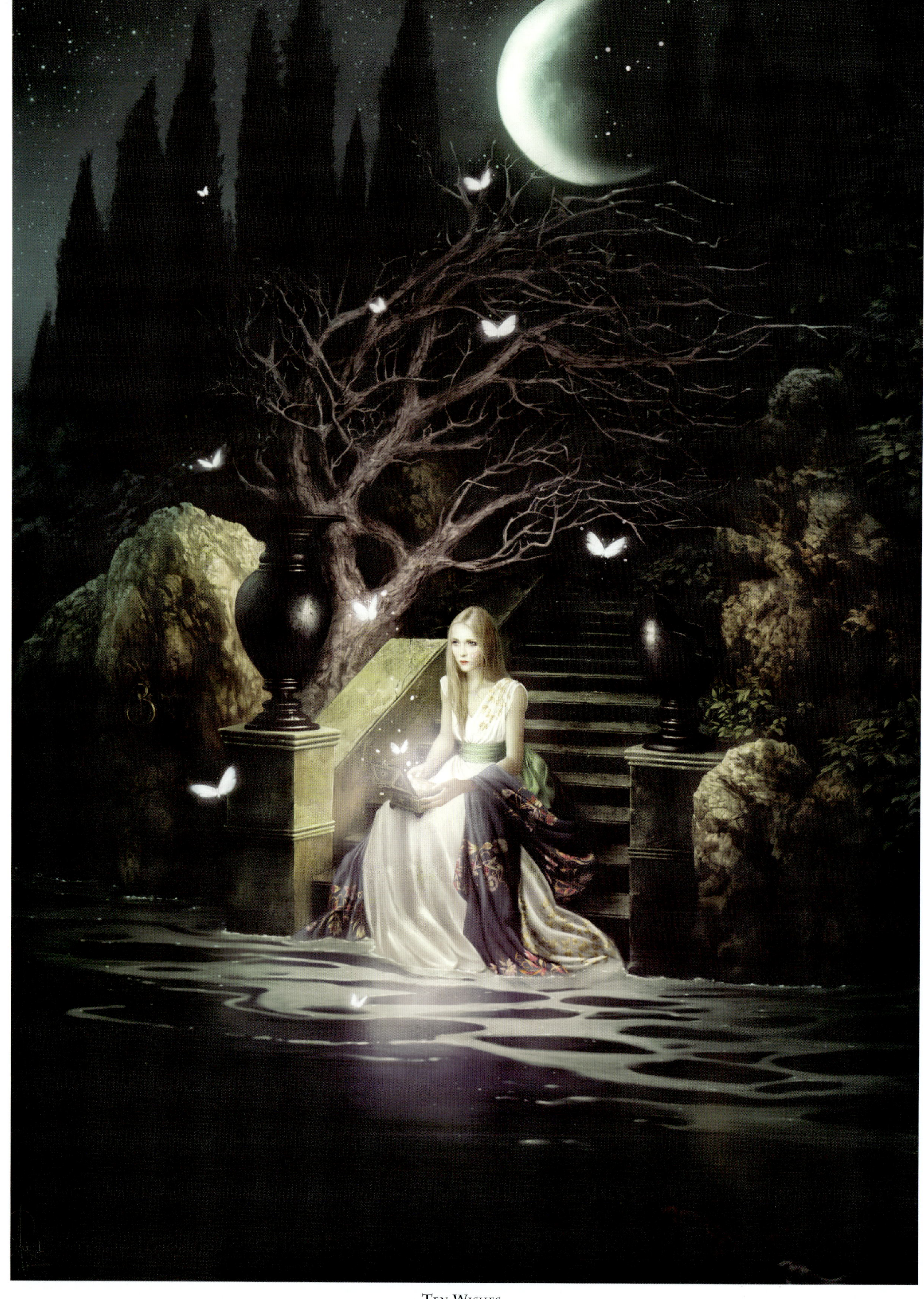

Ten Wishes

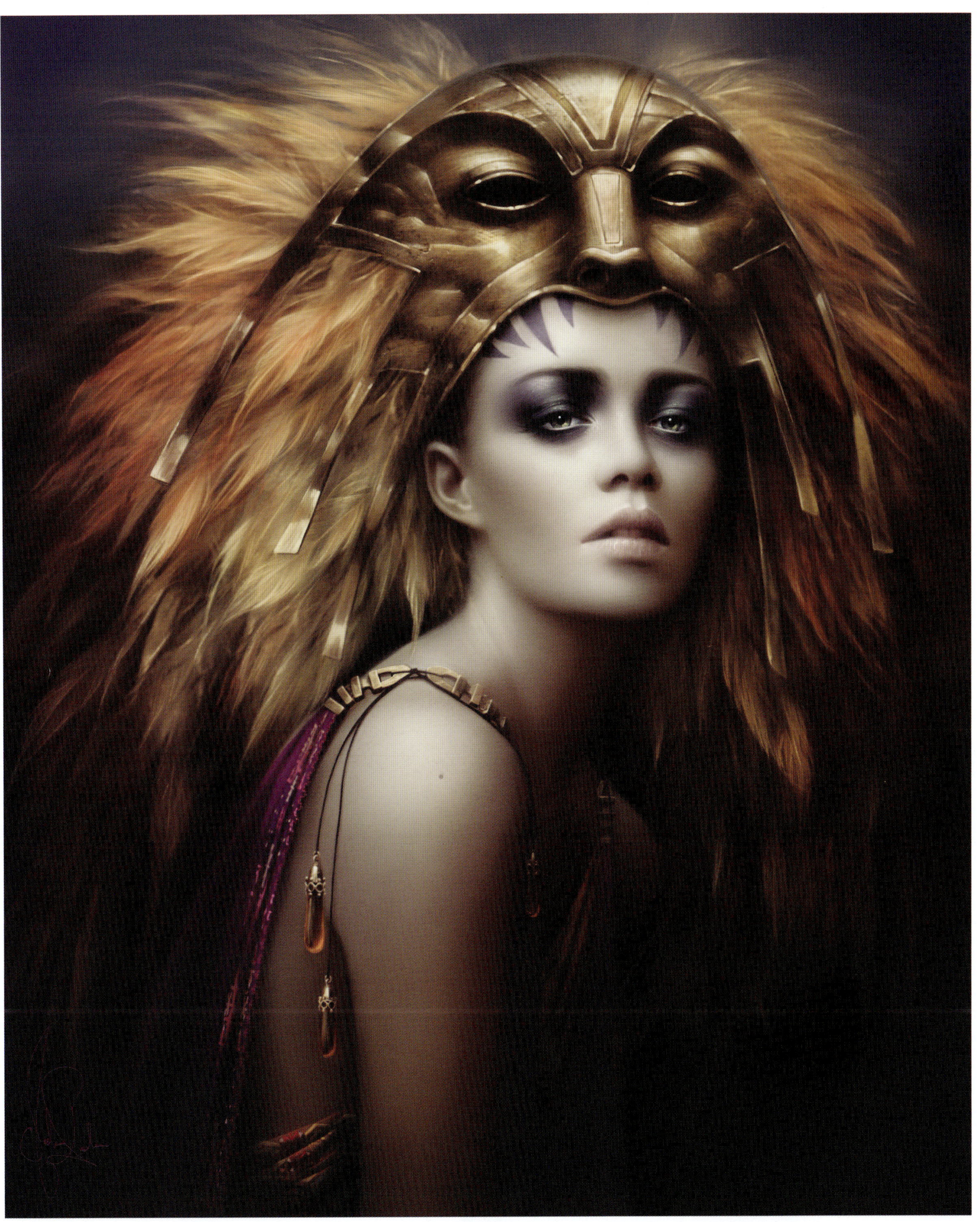

Magika

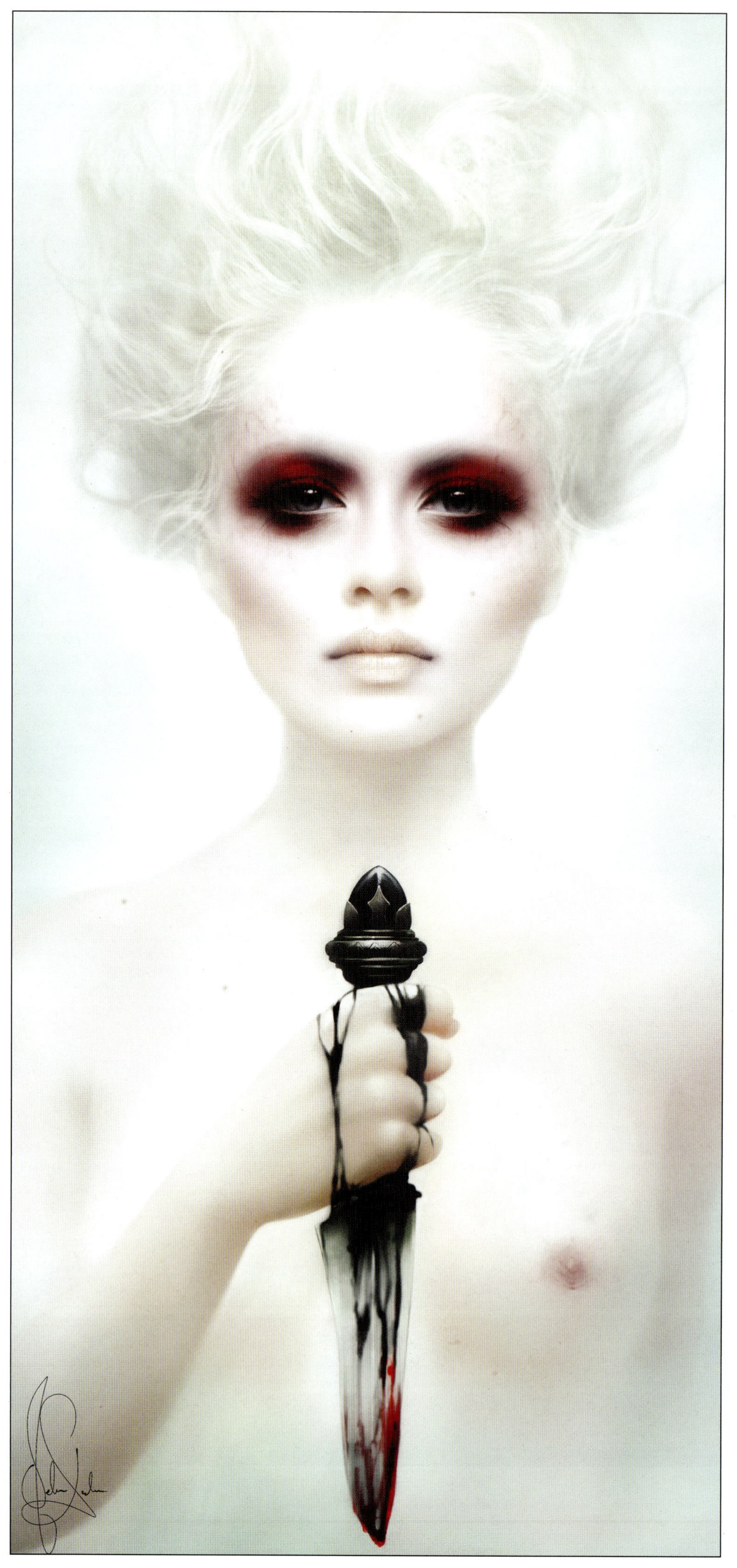

Infinite

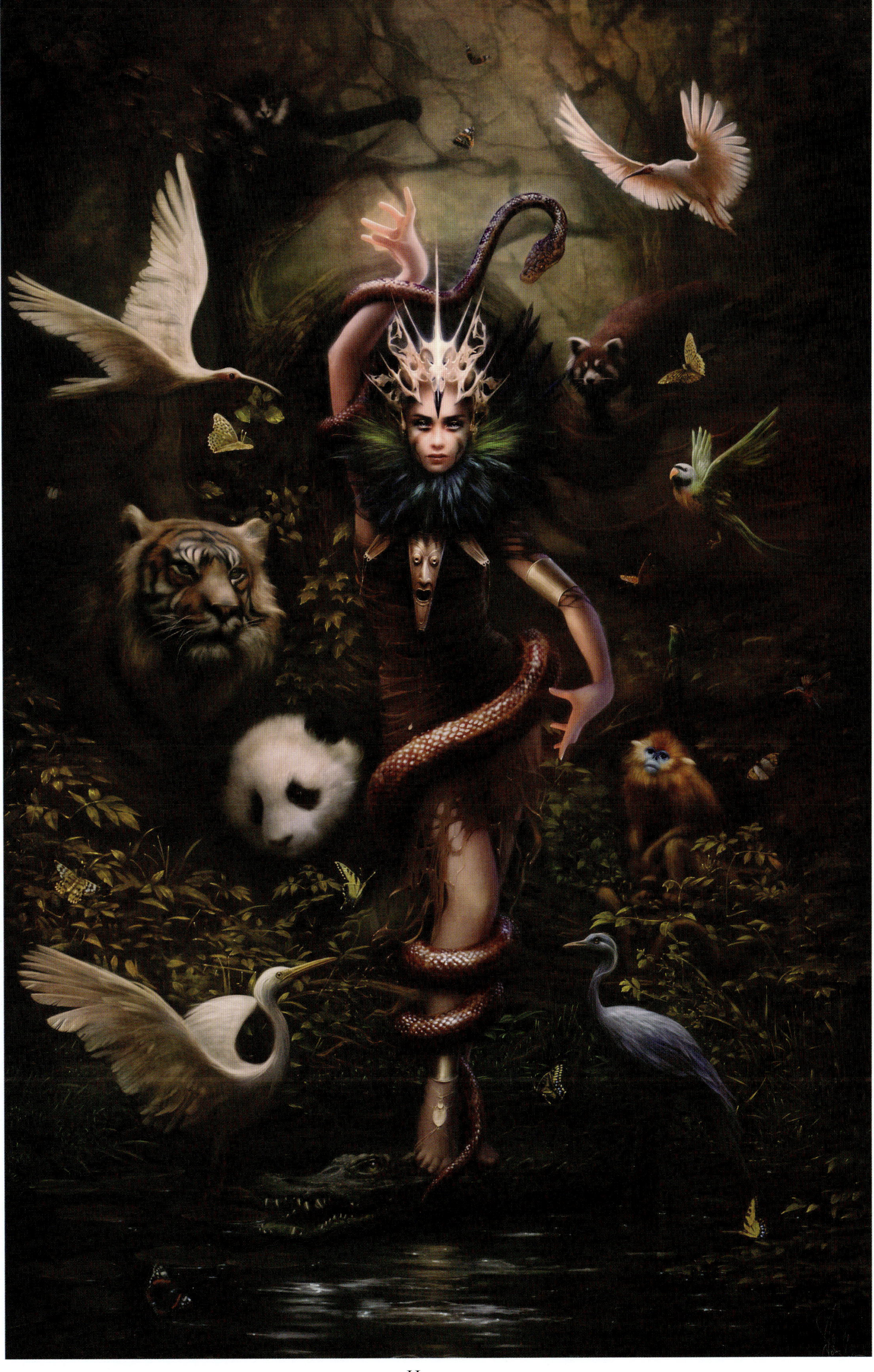

Harmony

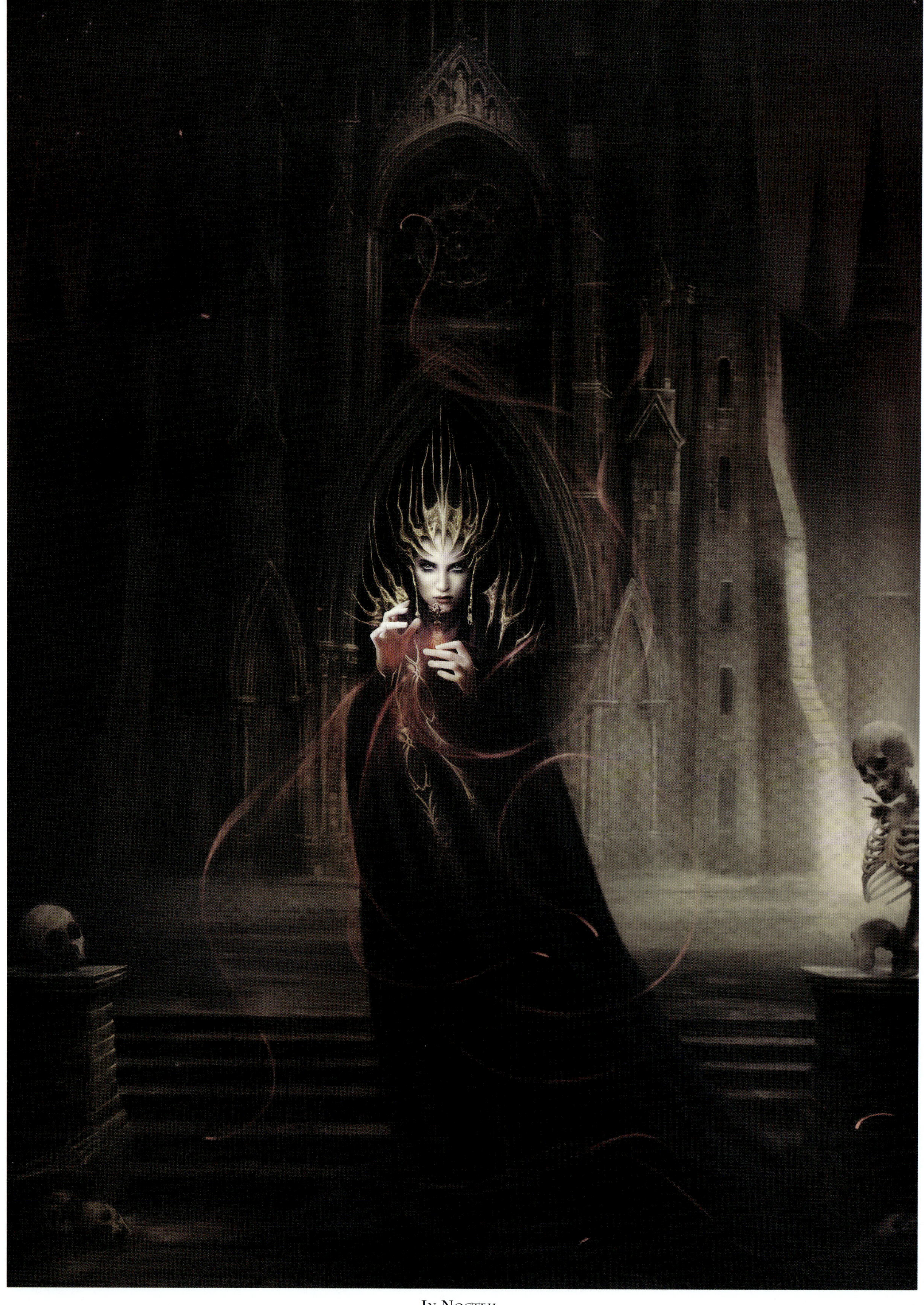

In Noctem

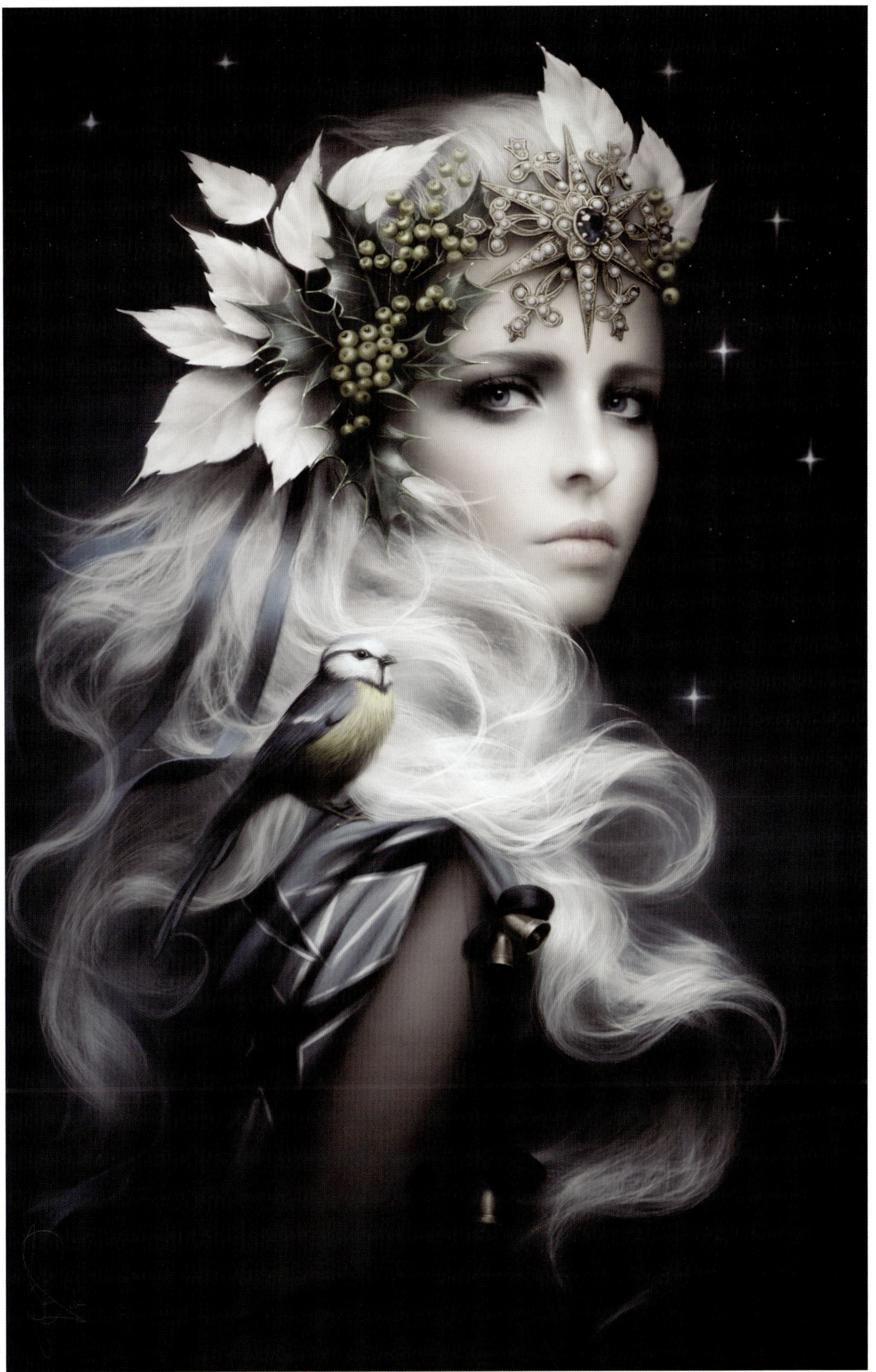

White

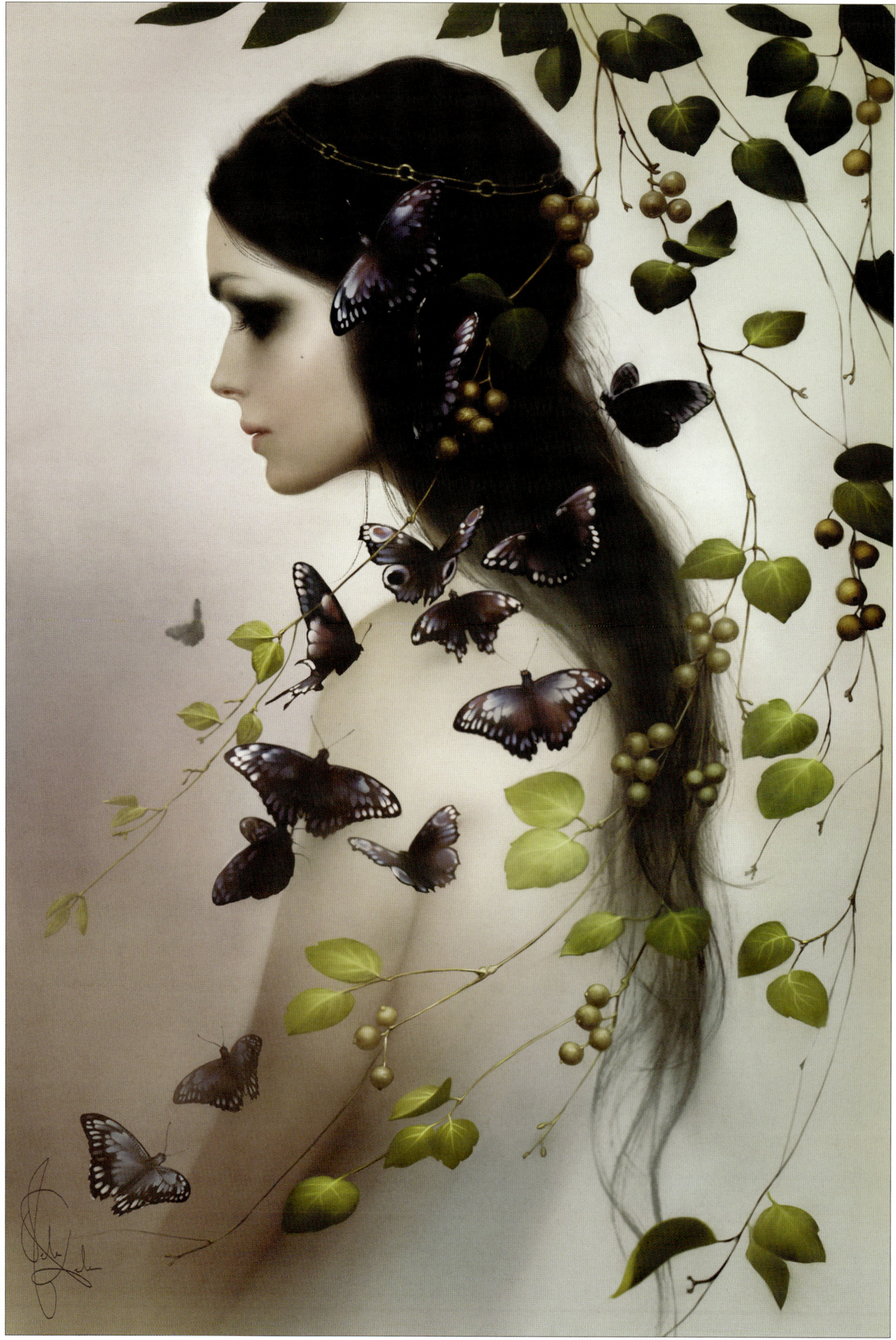

Mauve

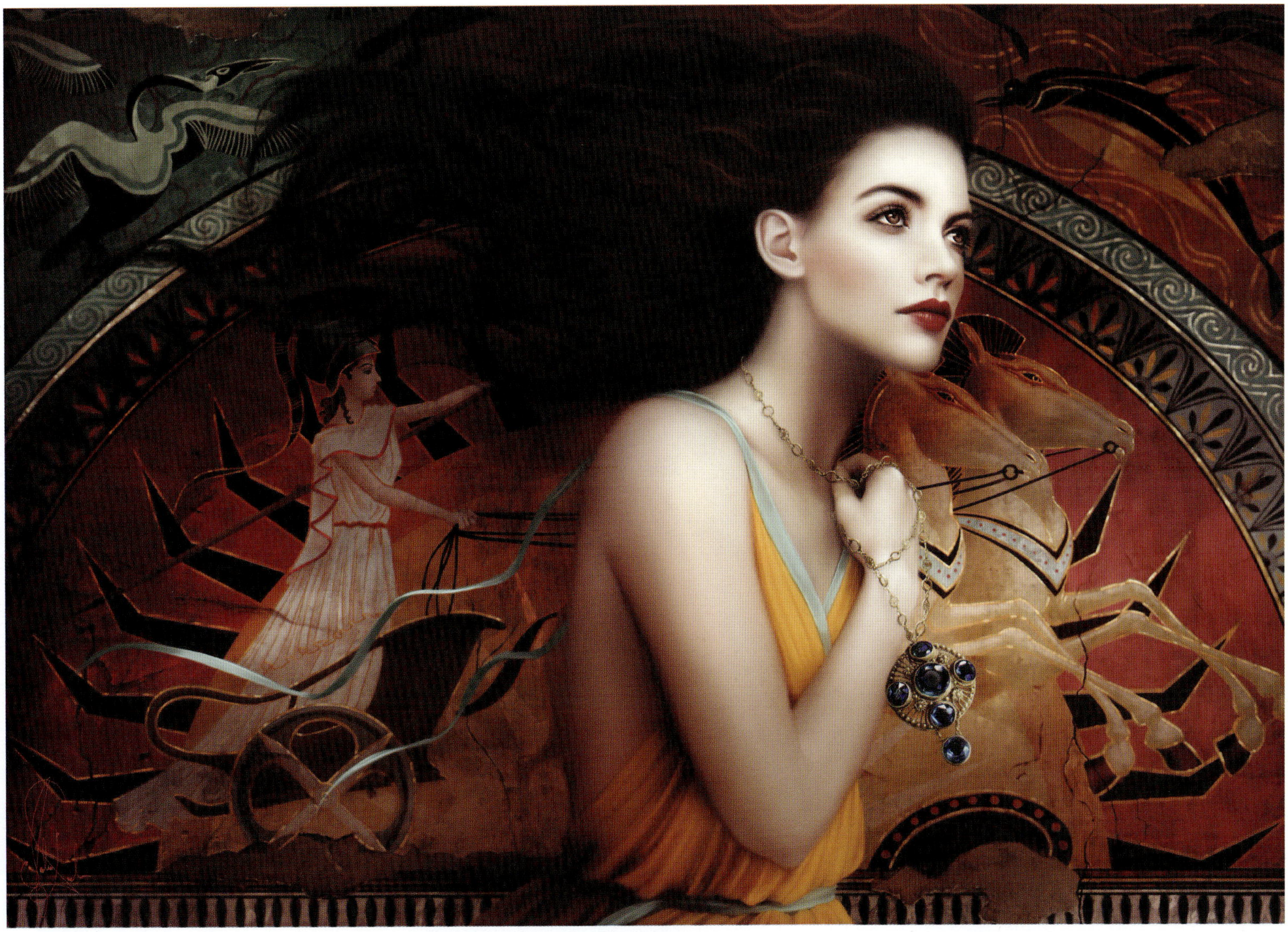

Up

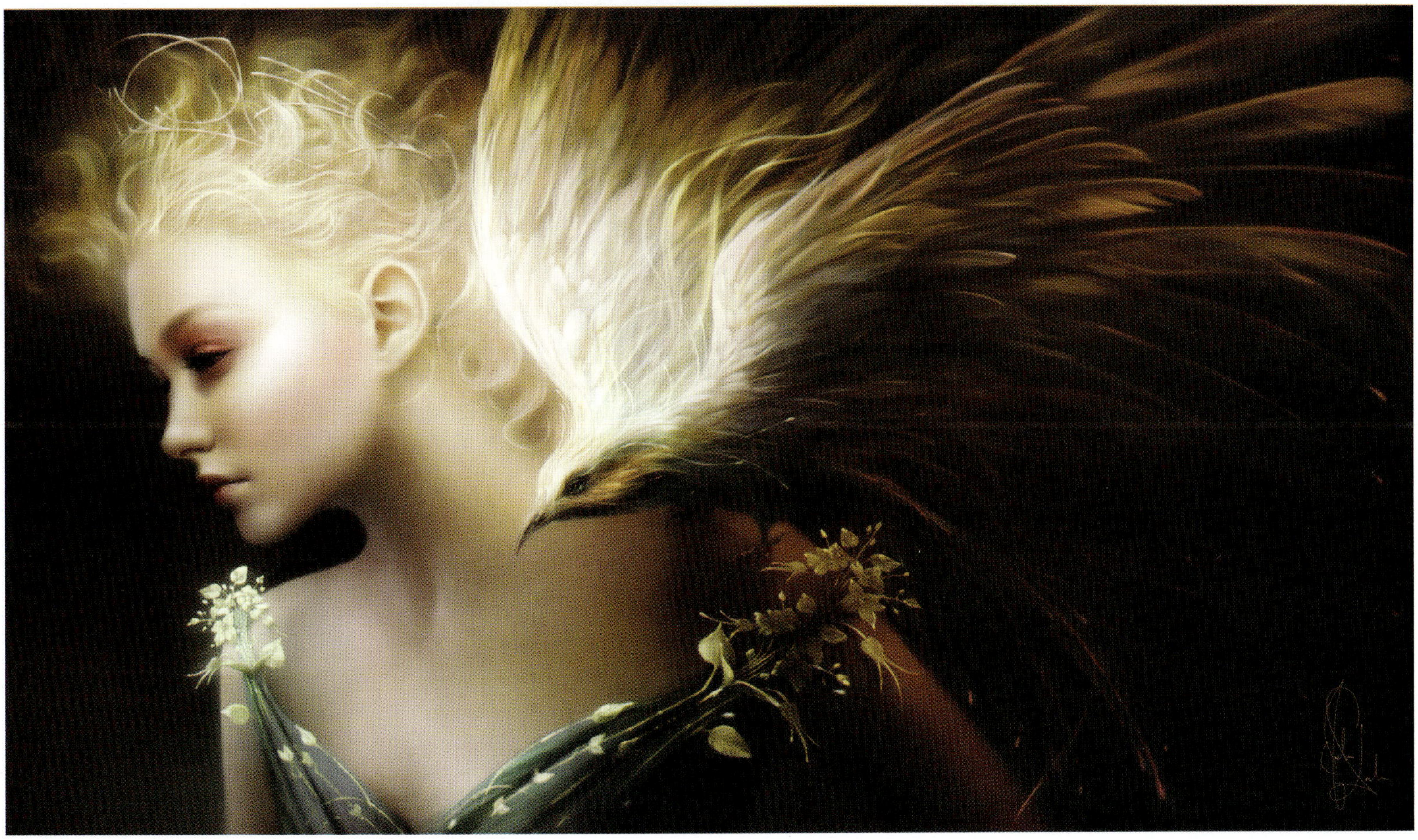

Sailor

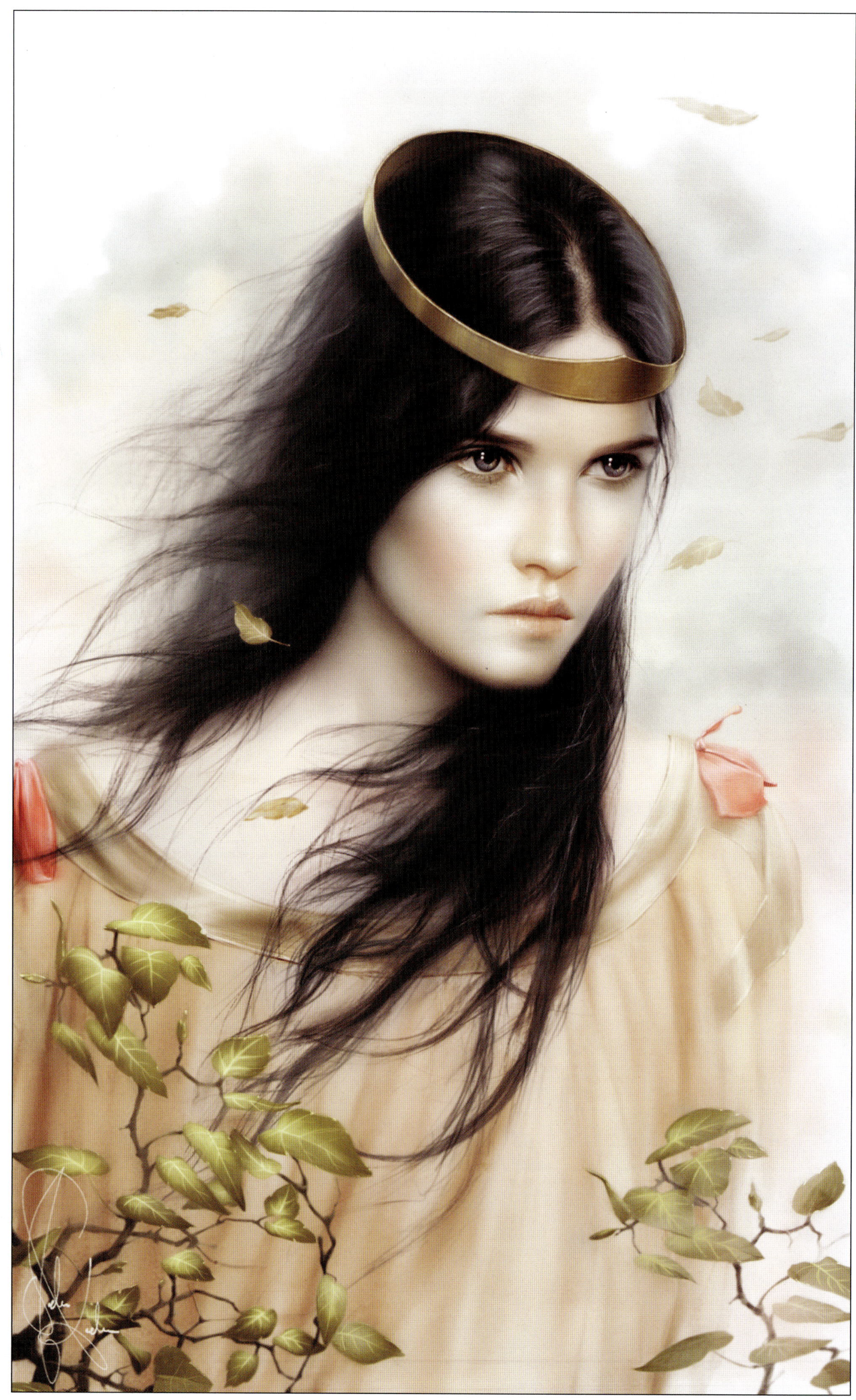

Apparition

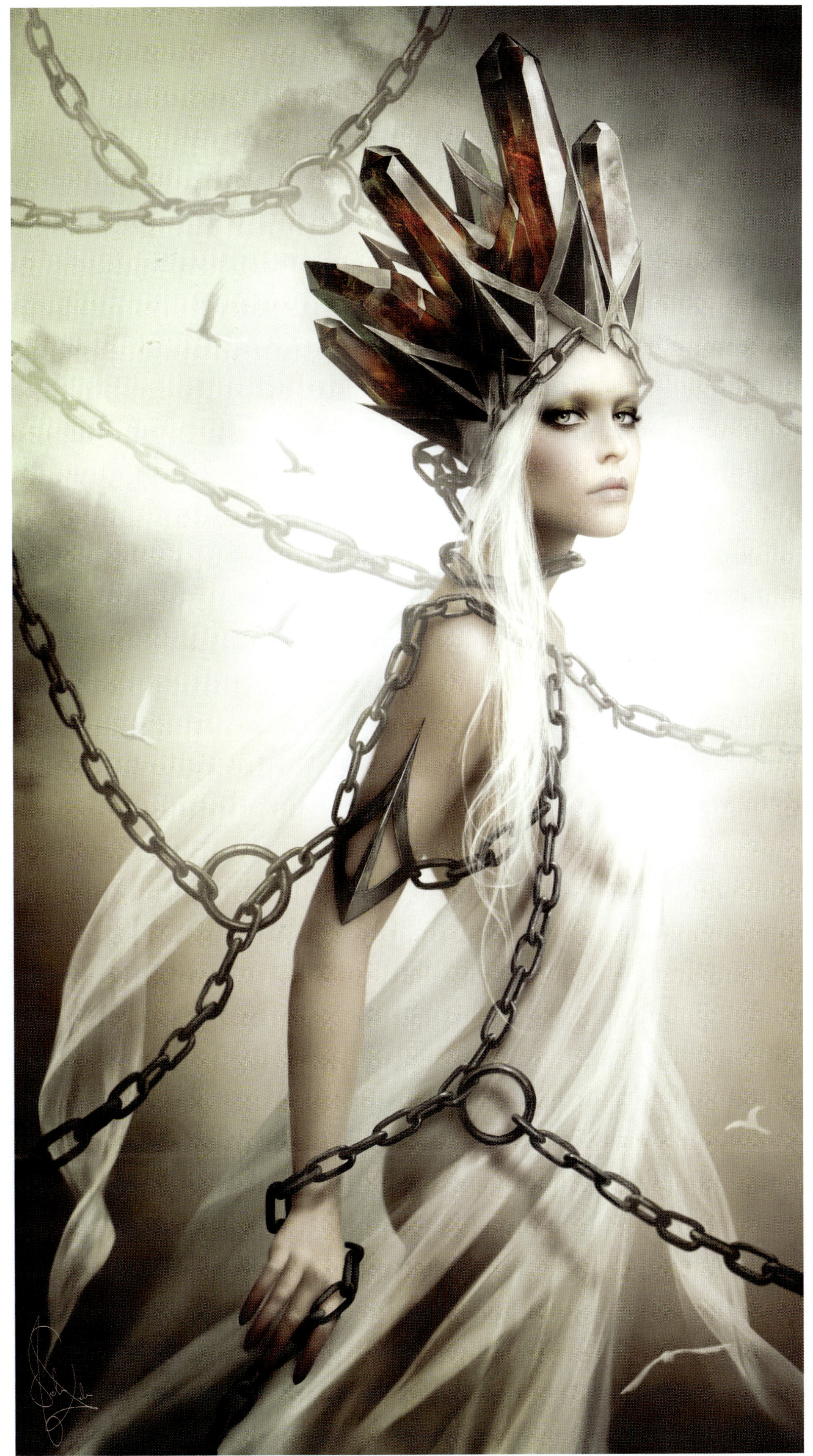

Elements

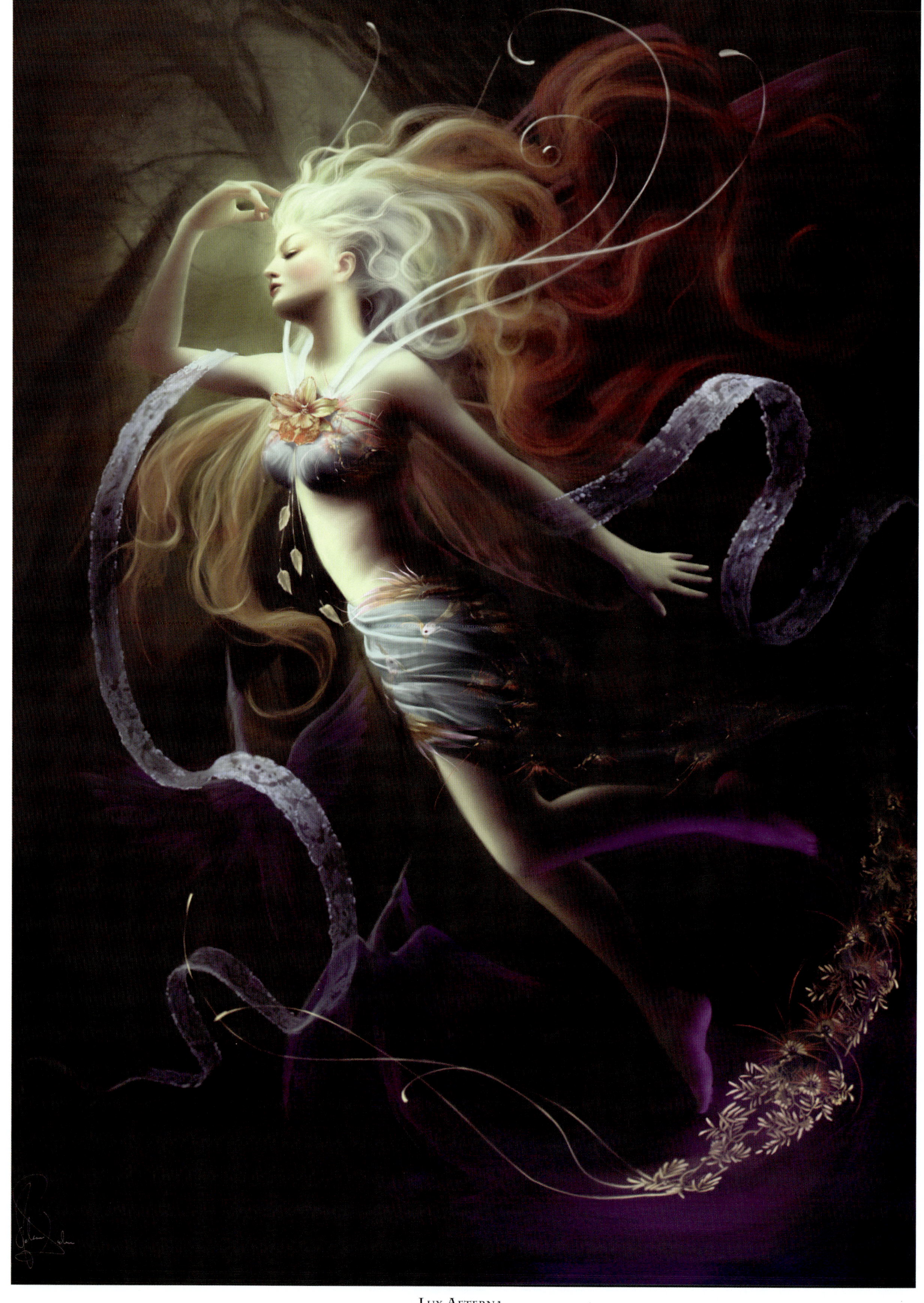

Lux Aeterna

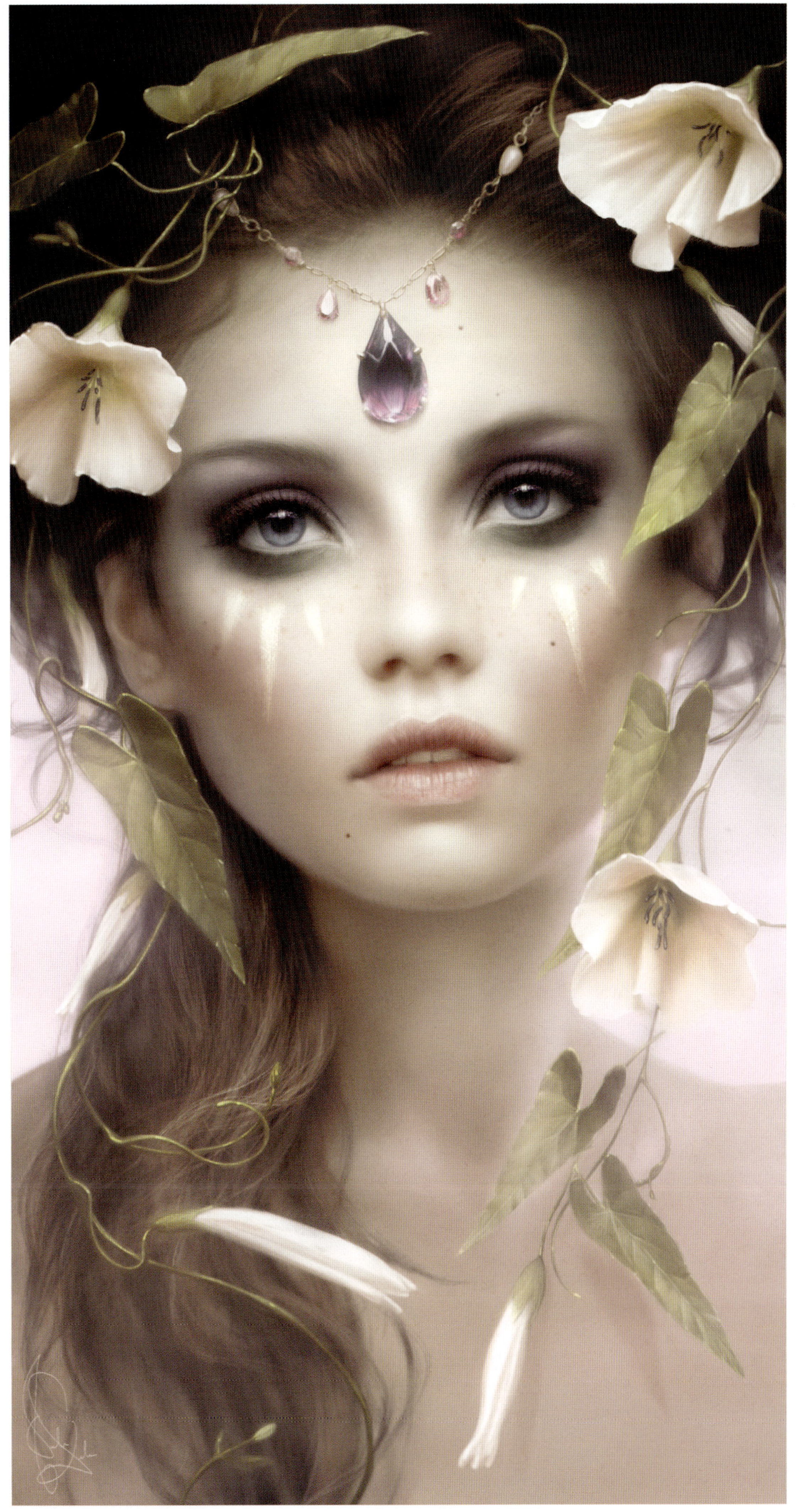

Euphoria

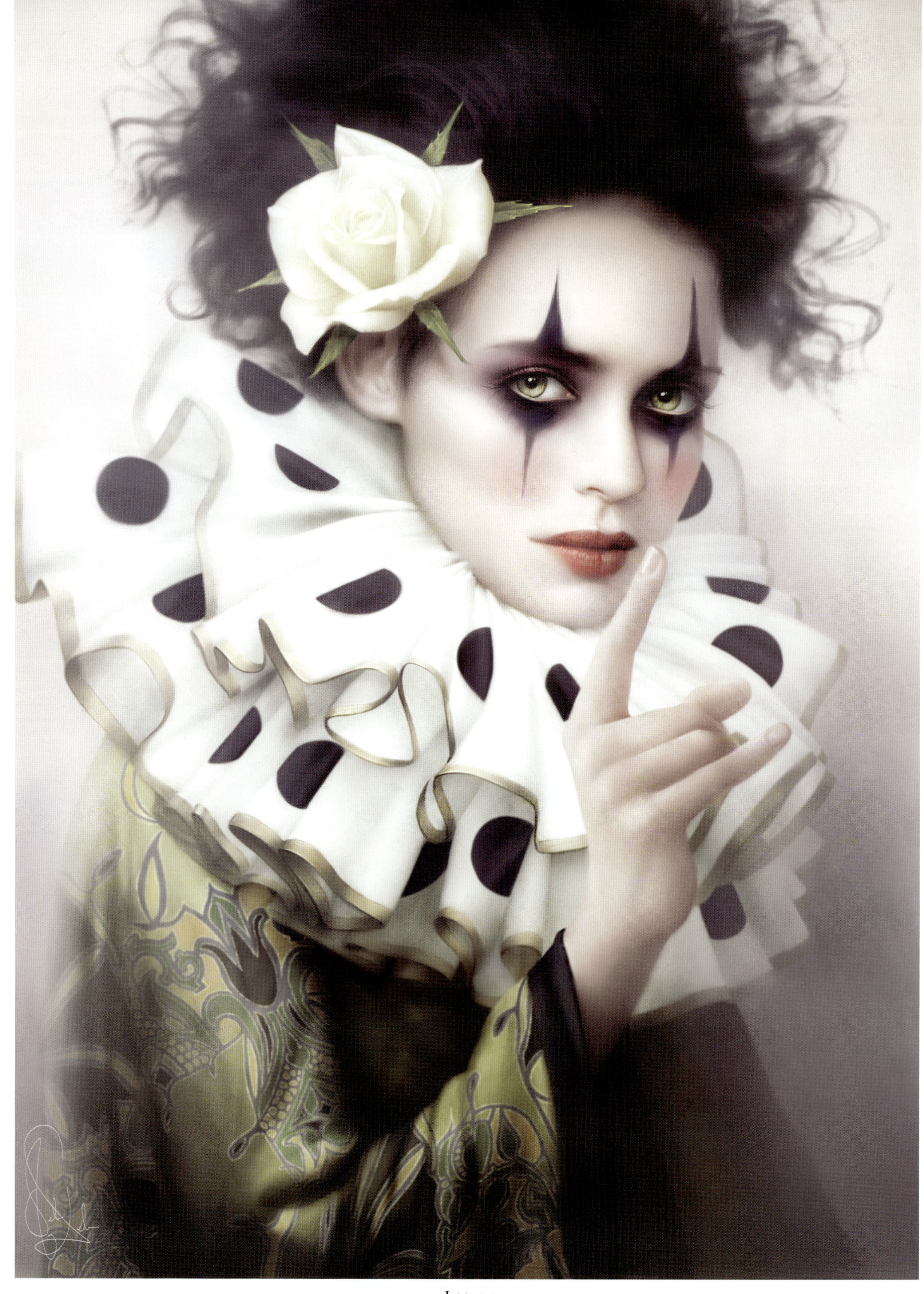

Lizzie

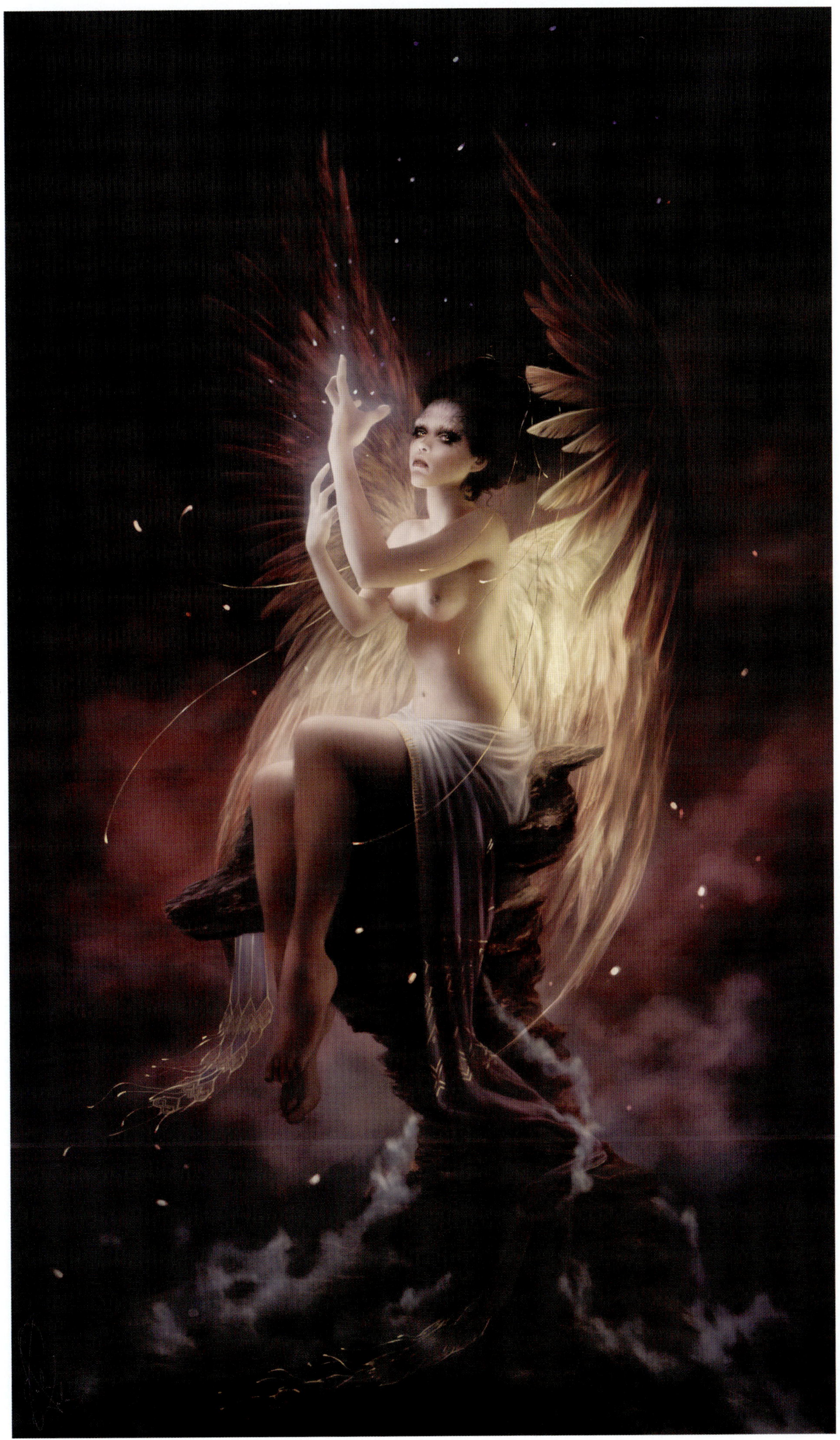

Eyes on Fire

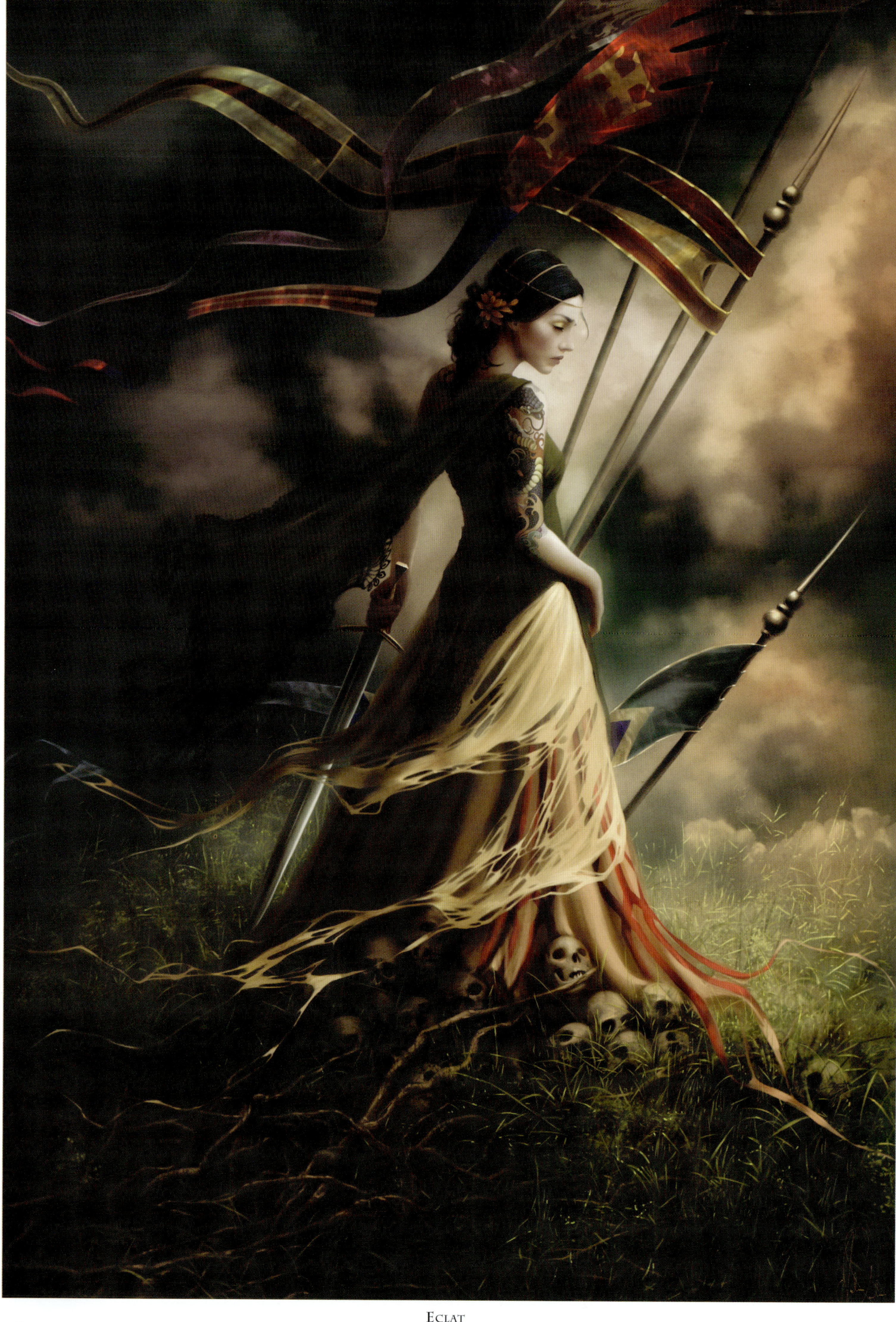

Eclat

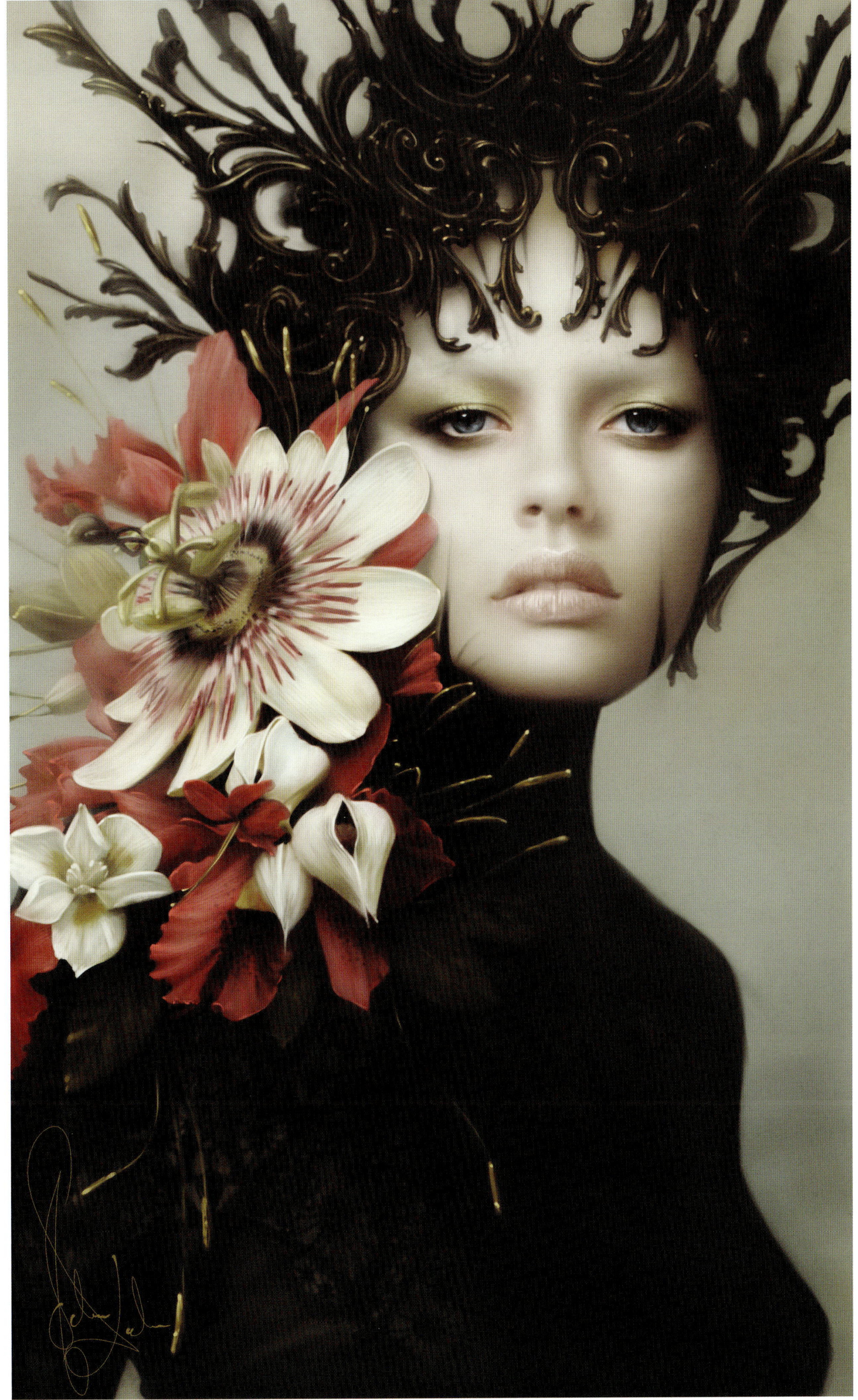

Circle

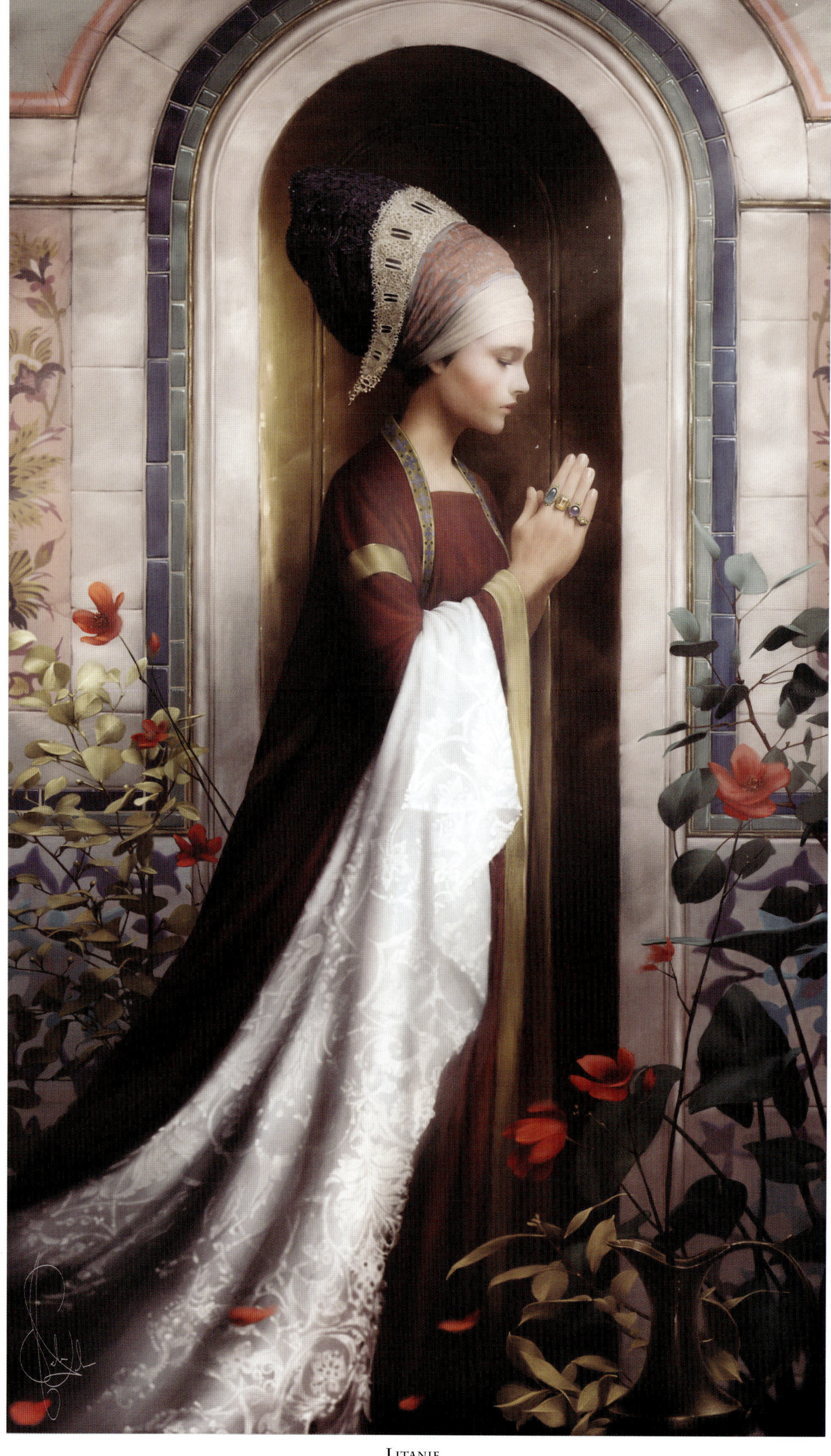

Litanie

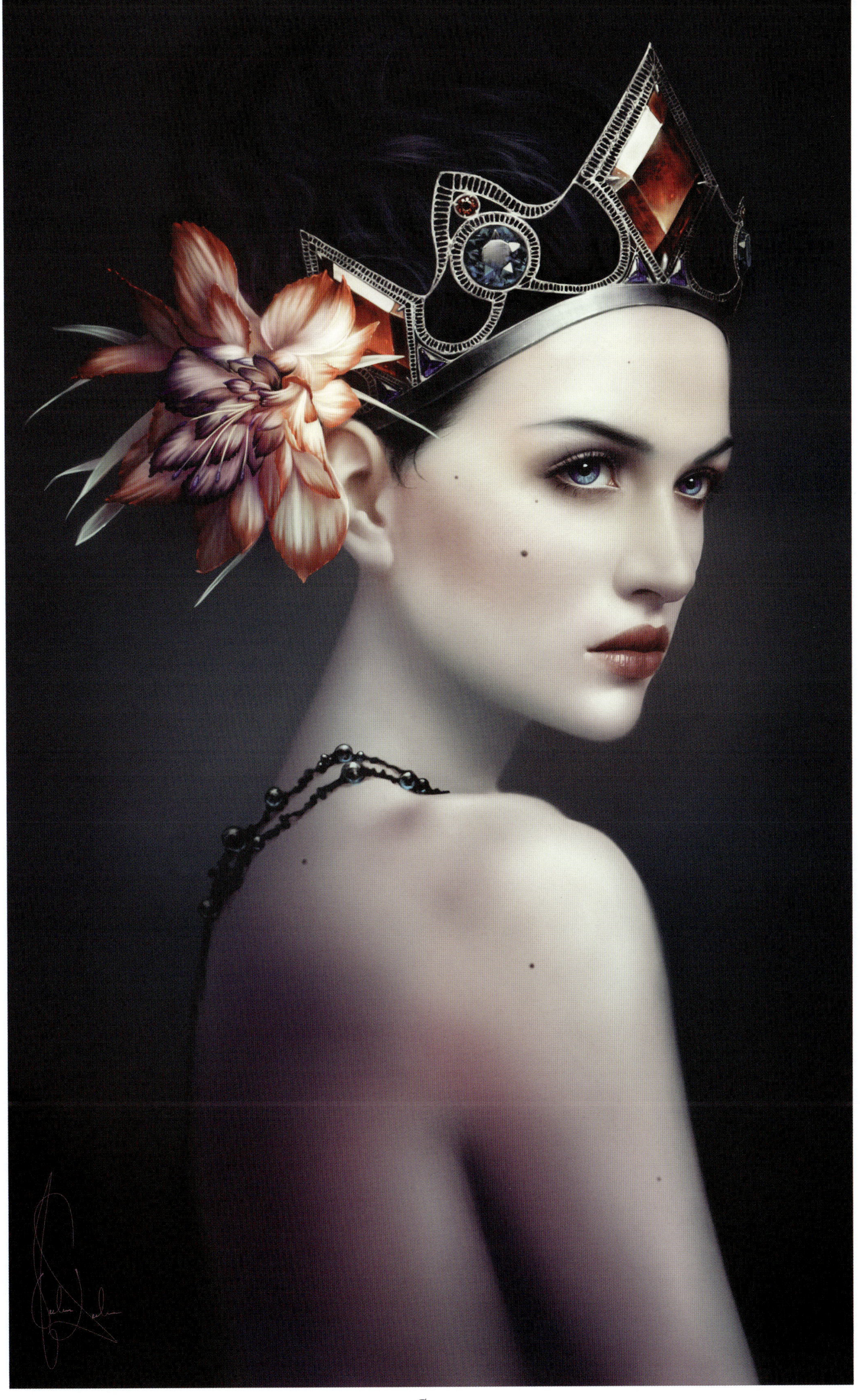

Cold

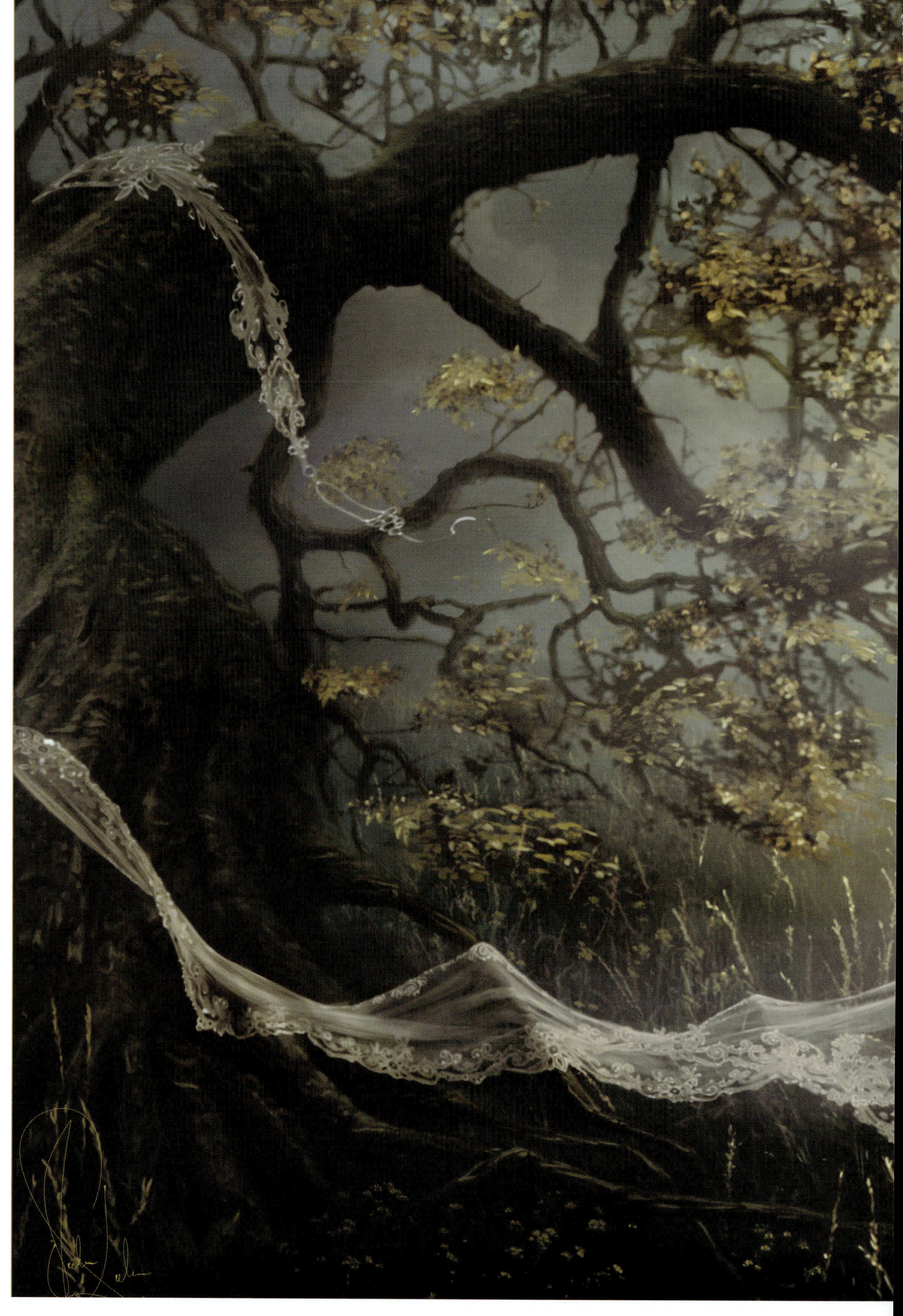

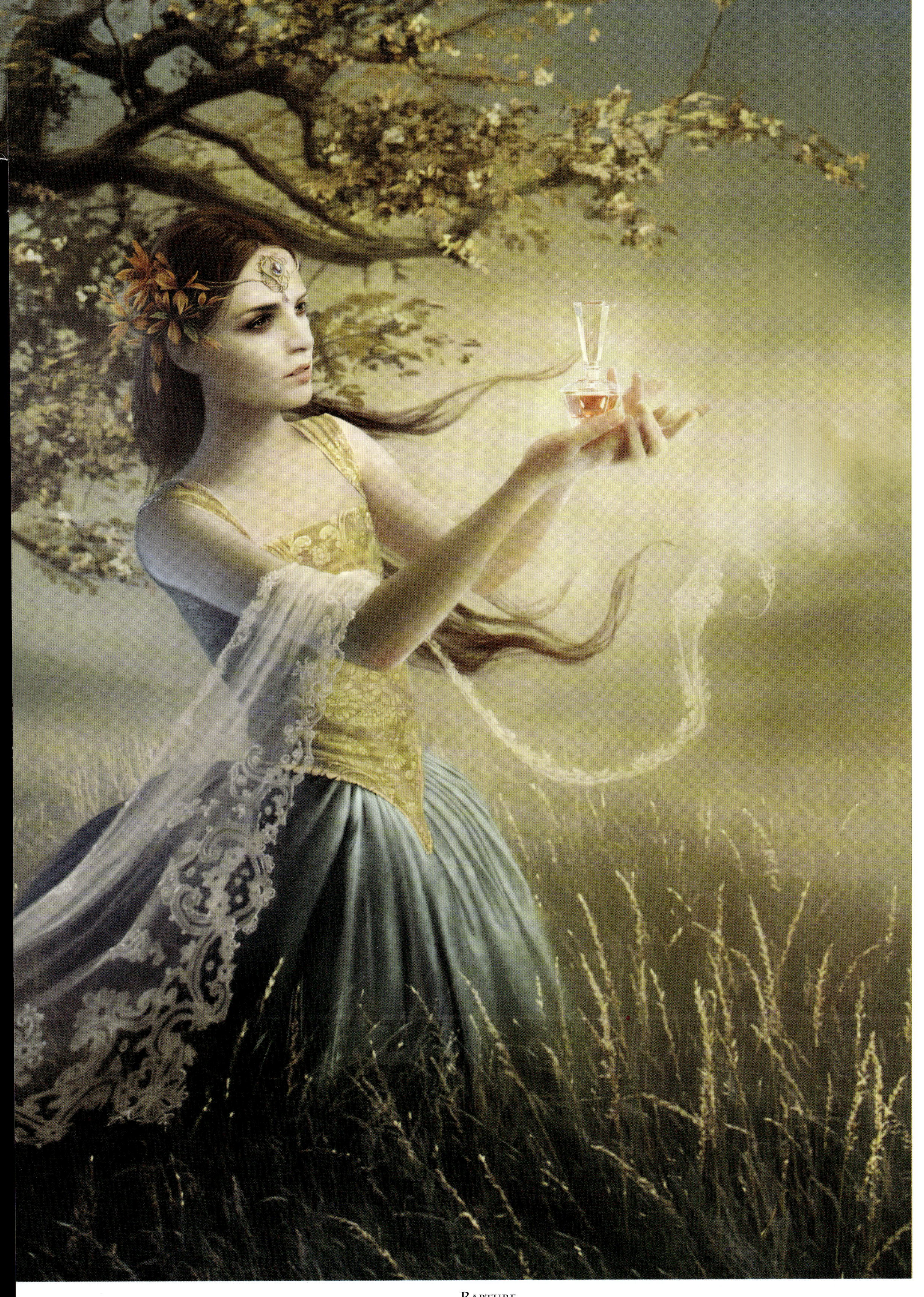

Rapture

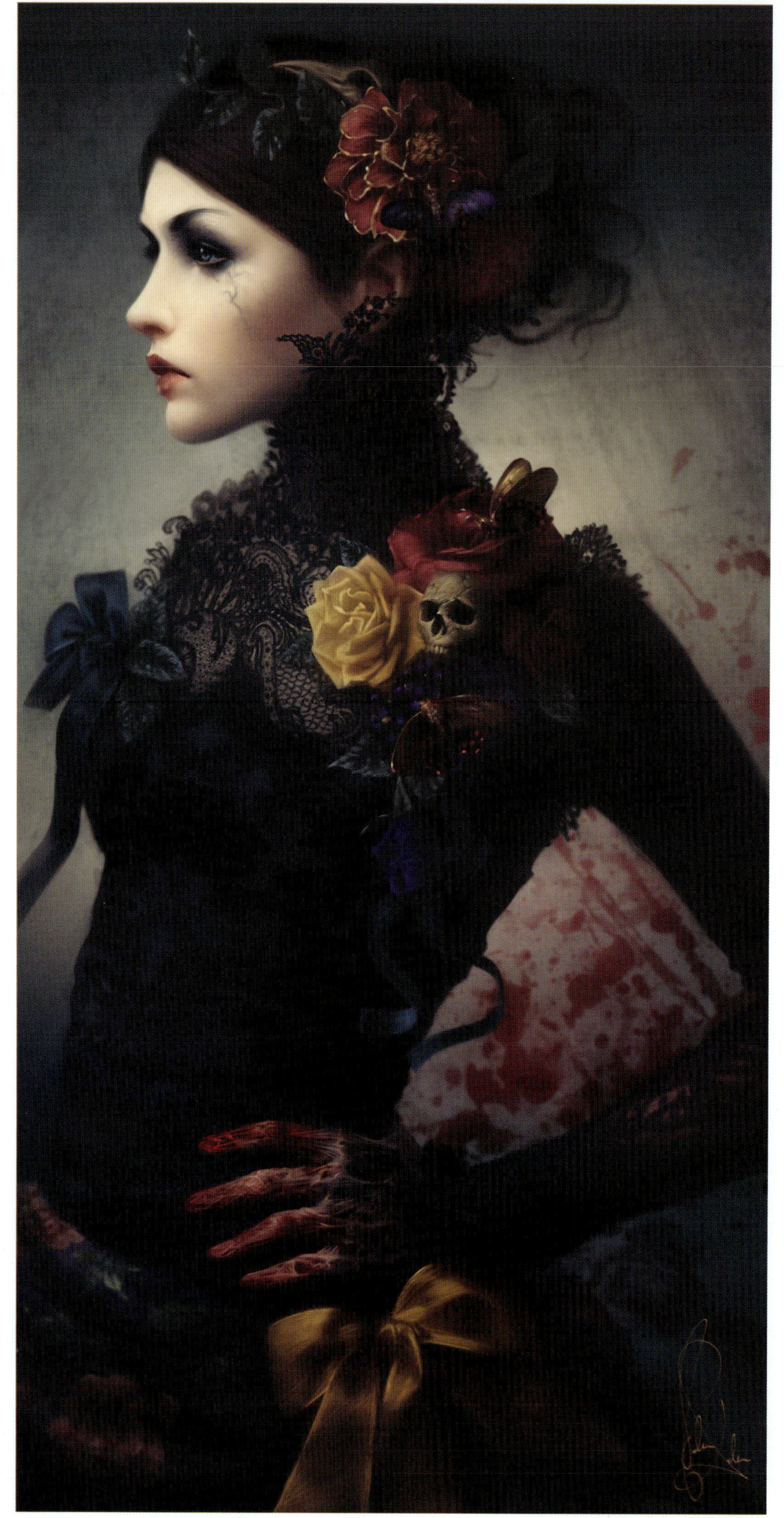

Violette

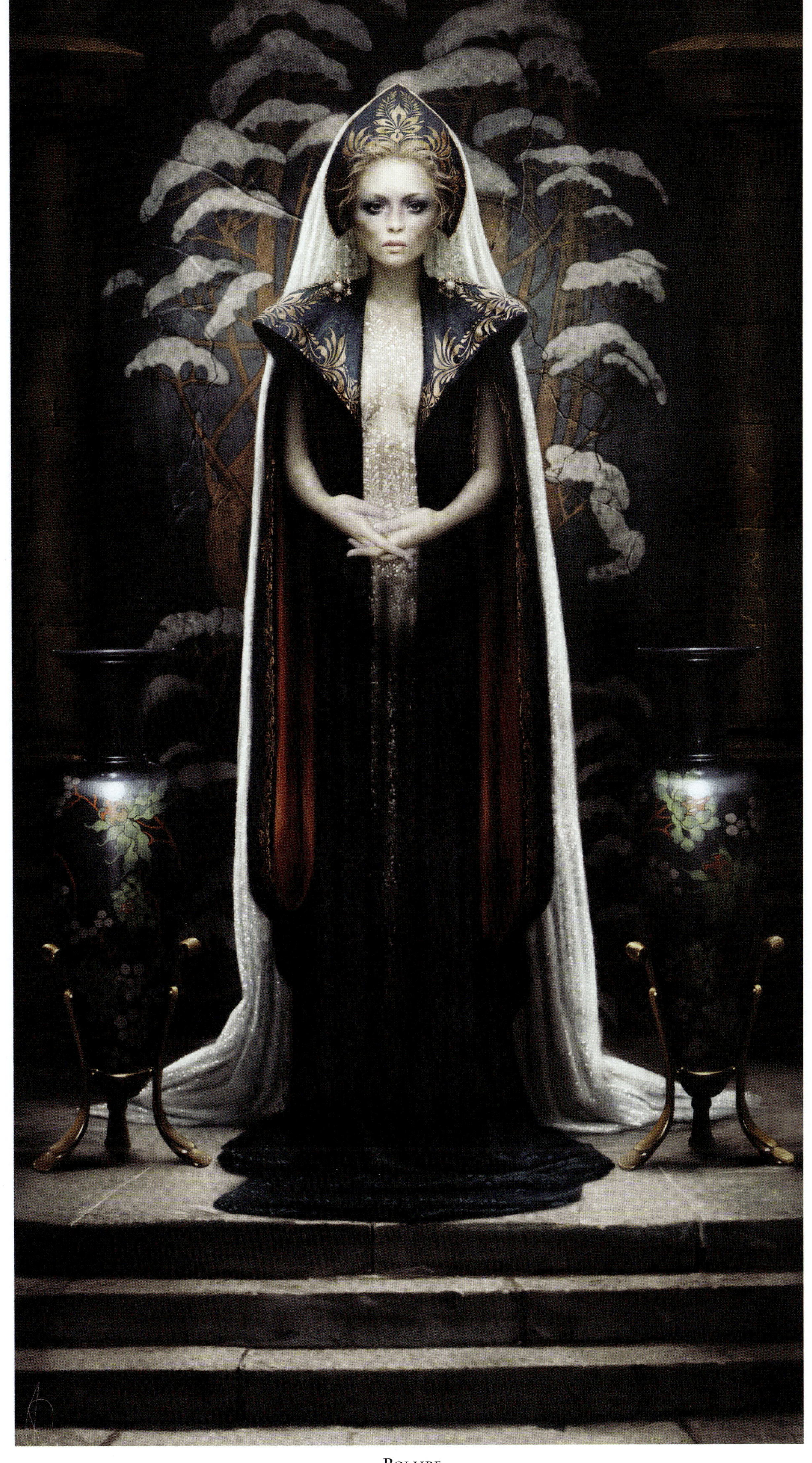

Polaire

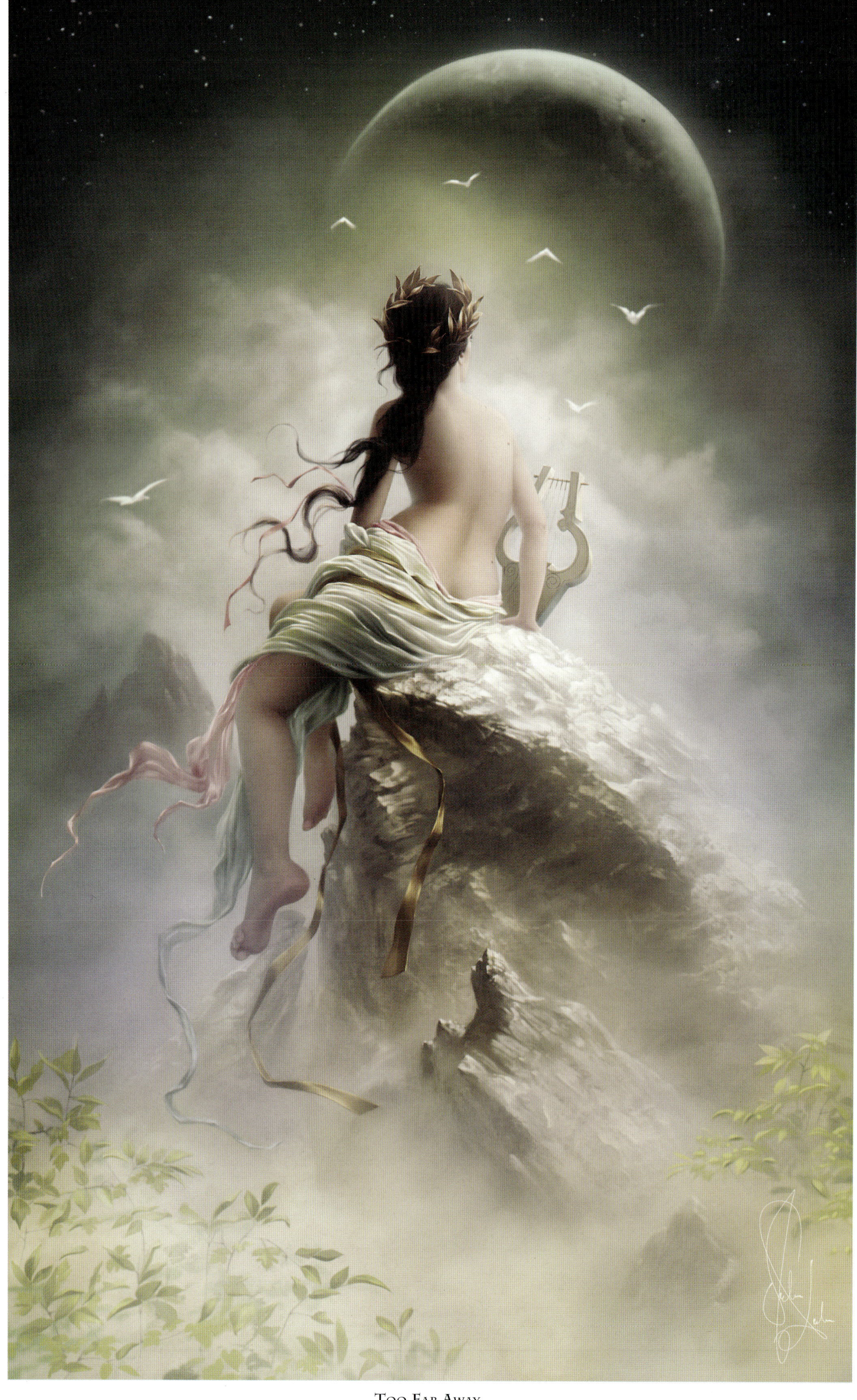

Too Far Away